The Lost Tales of Hong Kong

The Lost Tales of Hong Kong:

A Collection of Short Essays

Written by Siu Si
Edited and translated by Alice Cheng

ISBN 978 17 915 8642 3

Printed in the United States of America

First Printing: December, 2018

Table of Contents

Translator's Acknowledgments

The translator would like to acknowledge the kindness and generosity of the following people: Dr. Chan Yuen Sang; Mrs. Choi-Chow Yin Ping, and her husband, Mr. Choi Sung Kei; Dr. Chu Kin Wah; Dr. Ho Wing Lau; Dr. Alvin Kwok Kwan Ho; Dr. Gerry Kwok Gin Wai; Professor Lo Wai Luen; and Dr. Tam Wai On.

Prologue

Nostalgia should not be considered a trend, because it is a natural human tendency to yearn for people, events, and objects of the past, whether they were good or bad, right or wrong, beautiful or ugly. After all, experiences define our identity.

It goes without saying that we should not spend every single minute getting entangled in old memories. Still and all, occasionally a name, a street scene, a flavor ingredient, a phrase in the middle of a conversation, or a trivial incident in the depths comes to the surface before we know it. It is as vivid as real life. But when we reach for it, it becomes a sliver of an indistinct dream. There is no way to hold it in our hand.

We are travelers in a hurry. Only when we turn around do we see how far we have come on the journey, and how often we burst into laughter or tears along the way.

Retro is cool these days.

Let us not forget the past.

Let us remind ourselves that today was built on yesterday. When the warm, fuzzy feeling of nostalgia washes over us, we have a new perspective on failure, or, for that matter, success.

Let us tell ourselves there is no reason to take things too seriously. Just as we get tired of the hectic pace of life, it is time to pause for a moment, and to recall the sweet memories of the good old days.

Part I

Looking back on old memories,
We chit-chat with each other,
Never mind the lamp glows dimly,
Simple dinner, lots of laughter.
— Wang Anshi

"Toys"

I grew up in a deprived city during the war. Life was hard. As far as I can remember, I had nothing to show off to my friends. That said, I had three favorite "toys" from which I was inseparable until I started school at the age of nine. Why did I use quotation marks to enclose the word toys? It is because they were not meant to be objects for kids to play with.

The first "toy" was ants.

Ants are most resistant to adverse conditions. They are everywhere, even in places where humans survive on meager rations. Although there was not much to attract their attention in our house, black and yellow ants were seen constantly crawling from one corner to another. As they went on their way, they inevitably took a route along the balcony railings. Every day I ensconced myself on a low wooden stool, resting my forehead against the metal bars, and observed their troop movements with a keen eye.

Black ants are bigger. They have a slender waist but a protruding tummy. The stomach looks so bloated that it appears transparent especially when they drink too much water. They move their legs fast, but their formation is not tidy. Yellow ants are delicate and calm. They follow one line, and no one overtakes another. As an ant watcher, I found both species intriguing. Black ants were creative artists teeming all over the floor, but they confused me and made me scrunch up my eyes. Yellow ants presented a united front. The leader and the workers were easily identified. However, they were too conservative to unveil any new show. If I fixed my gaze on them for a long time, I would become cross-eyed.

Ants spent the whole day moving their eggs (which are white in color) and carrying food back to the colony. Presumably, the small things that they carried around in their jaws were food, but I was not really sure. The foraging behavior was a magnificent spectacle. A single black ant bit into the leg of a dead cockroach many times larger than its body, lifted it up effortlessly, and hurried away. However, if several of them worked together as a team to do their job, sometimes they lost their cool composure.

As their orderly way of foraging did not give me much excitement, I grew callous, really callous. To fix that lack of interest in their everyday life, I spritzed water on a chain of worker ants or squished one of them. Right away all I saw was this frenzy of ants running all over the place. And I just watched how they got organized in the aftermath of my attack. I think that, in retrospect, nature was allowed to take its course. But those poor ants I had killed died for no good reason at all.

My second "toy" was a pair of pill bottles.

In those days, the pill bottle was a small glass container typically cylindrical with a narrow neck. I used to keep two, one with a red cap and the other with a blue cap. They made a nice couple. As I was unaware of gender differences at that age, no decision was made on their sexes. During playtime, I removed them from a paper box. I unscrewed their caps, and balanced them on the mouths. Now the pill bottles looked like the back of two little fat men whose hats got askew.

In order to create the illusion that they were alive, I moved them up and down, and changed my voice to speak in their roles. Sometimes they spoke to each other; sometimes they spoke to me. (Naturally I do not recall the content of the conversation.) I cocked my head, rested my chin on the edge of the table to have my eyes on the same level as theirs, and started talking. They were my best buddies, but they had never been given a name.

My third "toy" was an island of Lilliput that only existed in my head.

I do not have the foggiest idea of how I hit upon such a wild idea, but it did not come from *Gulliver's Travels.* (I did not hear about the story until much later in my life.) I was home alone for most time of the day. Usually I sank into a wicker armchair on the balcony, and stared into the empty living room. Upon the floor, I formed a mental picture of streets, houses, cars, and pedestrians. Every day, a sequence of different events took place, but the scene remained unchanged. I was able to tell the types of shops that lined the street, and the quotidian activities of each pedestrian. I made sure that something happened in the street, and constructed a story based on that incident. (I was probably talking to myself again.) I do not believe that my ideas for stories came from anyone. My maternal grandma was the only person who told me stories, and the only stories she knew were from the classic novels *Water Margin* and *Romance of the Three Kingdoms*. Whatever the case might be, I was in good spirits when I assumed a commanding position in my wicker armchair, overlooking the teeny-weeny city on the floor.

Days turned into weeks, weeks turned into months, and months turned into years. Those were the "toys" I grew up with. They were not bought with money. Whenever I look back on those days, I cannot help but be thankful. I was home alone all day but not lonely. The war impoverished my family but the experiences of it had enriched my young life. I have nothing to brag about my childhood but I am proud of it. (Oops, I kept contradicting myself.)

P.S.: It was in the morning news that a rich kid jumped out the window when his parents were away. His lonely room was filled with playthings. The headlines reminded me that as a child, I drew the short straw, but it turned out that less was more.

April 27 – 28, 1994

Ten Good Old Things

Rattan School Bags

People my age all used a rattan briefcase to carry books when we went to elementary school. Yours was not nicer than mine, because they were two drops of water in the same bucket.

The woven case is made by crossing fine rattan strands under and over each other, which are not unlike tiles hung in parallel rows from the roof of an ancient house. Every part of the case is made out of rattan, including a pair of clasp locks that bolt the front shell to the back shell. However, to ensure that the edges are reinforced, the frame is crafted out of bamboo. As a briefcase is opened and closed frequently, the rattan bolt stick does not stand up to the wear users give it. The little stick is easily broken. In that case, we would use a single chopstick as a replacement to slide through the two clasp locks on the back shell.

Rattan withstands hard use. A rattan briefcase is most endurable and lasts for several years. When an elder son of a family went to junior high, he was entitled to a new one and passed on the old one to his sibling. It is generally believed that due to oils and moisture transferred from the human hand, the more a rattan briefcase is handled, the more its color becomes shiny, and the more its strands gain suppleness. When we were told that the hand-me-down was all perfectly shipshape, we swallowed it hook, line and sinker. Without a squeak of protest, we took whatever was offered to us. Sometimes an attachment point came loose, and strands became unwoven. If that happened, there was always someone in the family who knew how to fix it. A length of cotton string or rattan strand would be used to re-attach broken weave. However, if the job was not properly done, then we needed to be extra careful if we brushed by a fashion-forward woman in the street. We had no intention of causing her grief just because the rough surface of our case got caught on her expensive pantyhose.

The ultra-light rattan briefcase was a perfect school bag, except that it was not water-resistant. Rain would soak into books. That was the real problem.

May 15, 1980

School-Uniform Overalls

The elementary-school uniform I first wore was a skirt in navy. Later on, my school changed its uniform policy, and kids were allowed to wear overalls (I do not remember when it started). At any rate, elementary- and high-school students in Hong Kong all wore white shirts and blue overalls back in my day.

We usually got years of wear out of a pair of overalls. At the school's uniform shop, parents often reminded the tailor that the pant legs should be made looser, and the suspender straps longer. Ideally, the hem should be an inch or two below the ankle. Extra fabric was to be folded under and stitched down. As we grew taller, the suspenders were to be adjusted inch by inch to lower the pants. When that was no longer possible, the hem was to be undone. Like that, it would take a few years for us to grow out of a pair of overalls. Putting on weight, however, presented a problem harder to be solved. The thing is, if the pants are made too loose, they will not stay up. To ensure a fit for skinny ones, we wore pants framed by way of side adjusters, which are two strips of cloth brought together with a slide buckle. When we got bigger, we would simply loosen the adjusters. And if we kept getting bigger, we had no choice but to consider new uniforms – hurrah! Nevertheless, we all had to wait a couple of years before that day came. As for myself, I had stopped putting on weight for more than a couple of years – just my luck! Since Mother had given the tailor specific instructions that my pants were to be made a few sizes bigger, the blue uniform always hung from my body like a potato sack.

Overalls are comfy, except that narrow shoulders sort of spoil the way they hang. The strap is liable to get loosened if the metal piece of the suspenders slides down. And that made me quite ill-at-ease. The moment a strap slipped off the shoulder, I hastily pulled it up.

May 27, 1980

Wooden Clogs

Getting a new pair of wooden clogs was a big day of my young life, because Mother decided that it was the only one occasion where my opinion counted. While leather slippers that people regularly wore around the house did not vary much within categories, wooden clogs came in all the different colors of the rainbow.

In Wan Chai District on Hong Kong Island, there were several shops that sold wooden clogs. On tier after tier of wooden wall-shelves, dozens of clogs – usually for women – were displayed. Floral designs painted in bright red and bright green on the surface of clogs were all impressively dazzling. By contrast, unpainted clogs in the natural color of wood with straight sides were for men. Plain and boring, they failed to catch my attention even if they were laid out in the place of honor. Inside the shop, there was a solid countertop. Customers first chose a pair of unfinished soles. Then the shop owner or his assistant would get the clog size before he nailed a leather strap onto the sole on the countertop. He did it quick, and made no error of judgment at all.

Clogs are taking a little while to wear in, as there is something peculiar in their design, which is, the rocker-bottom sole. Since the bottom of the toe spontaneously curves up when the foot is propelled to roll forward, the wearer shuffles his feet in a cripple-walk fashion. Thankfully, the problem will eventually go away. Come to think of it, clogs are not comfort shoes. In fact, what I actually miss is the time I went clog shopping with Mother.

May 27, 1980

Sarsi

When I was growing up, the Connaught Aerated Water Company was still doing business. One of its products was Connaught Orange Squash. However, Father preferred Sarsi created by A.S. Watson's. He often bought one and shared it with me whenever he took me window-shopping (we often shopped till we dropped).

Warning: It took much skill to drink a Sarsi!

When it was opened, a plethora of bubbles rose immediately. In double-quick time, I tipped the bottle gently so that foam would not flow out of it. Once the dark brown soda was poured into a glass, it frothed up enthusiastically. The taste of the first gulp was elusive. Some of the bubbles broke apart into tiny water droplets spraying me in the face. Those that did not burst became a little moustache of white foam staying on my lip – it was such good fun. "My, you chug down a Sarsi free and easy as if it were beer," Father exclaimed. How nice to behave like an adult and, even better, a free and easy adult! From then on, one of the things I always looked forward to was to open a Sarsi and take that first gulp. I was hoping I would leave a moustache of froth on my upper lip, which made me look like a free and easy adult!

However, if I had overdone it, I would choke on a mouthful of Sarsi. The moment I swallowed it, the bubbles started rushing upward. It made my lungs feel tight. I needed to wait until I was able to release a long burp. Then, gas surged up, passing swiftly from the stomach through the mouth. Right away chest pressure was relieved. Oh well, he that would have eggs must endure the cackling of hens.

June 4, 1980

White-Sugar Sponge Cake

Mother usually did not allow me to eat any snacks between meals, a few kinds of pastries that killed my four o'clock hunger pangs excepted. They included Chan Yee Jai's adlay cake and snow cake, and a street vendor's white-sugar sponge cake. They all were white in color and had a taste of sweetness. I had a preference for white-sugar sponge cake, not because it tasted better, but because it gave me a special kind of enjoyment.

In summer, my eyes were always heavy with sleep when the sun-baked street stretched away quietly in the afternoon. Around three or four o'clock, a vendor habitually appeared. Balancing a rattan tray of white-sugar sponge cake on the head, he started chanting loudly in a slow drawl: BAAK – TONG – GOU. The word gou 'cake' was barely choked out. All kids were thrilled at the prospect of a treat. At his usual slot, he stopped over, opened a wooden stand with foldable legs, and placed the tray over it. He would not be there all day, though. So, we frantically tried to make our mothers aware that the vendor had shown up. Mine did not give the nod every time, but if she did, I would fly out of the house as fast as I could. The piece of cake with a soft, glossy finish in my hand was worth every one of the ten cents I had paid him. What could be easier to beat the heat on a drowsy day than that?

June 4, 1980

Amboyna Furniture

Furniture made out of amboyna wood is solid and looks respectable. It is ideal for the living room.

A round amboyna dining table, which came with four round stools, was centered in the living room of my childhood home. Upon closer examination, the marble inlay tabletop displayed the characteristic swirls and veins of the rock that bore a resemblance to murky cloud and hazy mist in Chinese landscape painting. Since the dining set had convex curved legs, the dark color of wood showed a unique depth and liveliness that created an eye-catching glimmer. A little amboyna tea-table, flanked by a matching pair of high-back chairs, stood on the left against the wall. The backrests of the chairs, decorated with wood carvings of the floral pattern, glinted. There was an enormous amboyna daybed placed on the right against the wall. The surface of the furniture, uncarved, shone softly, because daily use had smoothed it over in time. It also served as my bed. In summer, the amboyna bed was cool to the touch, but the downside was that it was rather unyielding beneath my stick-figure body. The bones cracked a lot when I was tossing and turning and counting sheep.

As things went, Father believed that furniture covered in dust was a total eyesore. The onus was on me to get ours dusted off three times a day, and waxed and polished once a week. On every Saturday afternoon, I applied a coat of wax to the surface of the furniture, then gently buffed and polished away all streaks and smudges. It was so satisfying to impart a lustrous sheen to the wood that I even felt a sense of indescribable bonding with the household items that I used to do the job. I had taken the chore out of waxing!

June 10, 1980

Wicker Armchairs

A chair made out of wicker is lightweight and elegant. It creates the ambience for relaxing, and brings some holiday charm to your home. It is the ultimate option for the patio and the balcony.

There were two big wicker armchairs on our balcony. Their deep golden sheen testified to the length of time that they had been in use. Over time, the seat had flattened from wear and tear. As a result of which, the pair looked more like two huge baskets for a little kid to hide in. From time to time, the wrapping on the armrest or the leg became unwoven. If the occasion arose, a handyman would be called in. His job was to replace the broken strands with new ones. Once repair work was done, the new strands never blended in with the armchair because of their noticeably paler color. For that reason, a recently-fixed armchair was dubbed a "Tuxedo Cat" in my family.

While the design of a high-back amboyna chair encourages the human body to adopt the perfect posture, there is no such thing as proper way of sitting as far as the wicker armchair is concerned. Usually I sat with my legs tucked under me. Sometimes I lounged on it, or put my feet on the other armchair. Boy was it relaxing! During the long summer vacation, I spent most of the time reading a book or dozing off in the armchair. For the rest of the time, I just settled in, rocking myself a little, and listening to the sound of its creaking. Then, before I knew it, a day had passed.

June 10, 1980

Radio Programs

Today, kids' entertainment is mainly watching television. If it is the case, I may as well say that mine was listening to the radio.

I did not particularly enjoy listening to Radio Hong Kong, as it was only on-air for a short period of time during the day, and most of its programs were uninteresting. We had a vintage radio at home. Father had used a bamboo pole (instead of a mount pole) to install an antenna on our roof so that we were able to listen to a radio station in Guangzhou on the Mainland. After ten o'clock in the morning, I usually tuned in for nanguan operas performed by blind musicians, which included full-length stories such as *History of the Eastern Zhou States*, *Untie a Red Satin Sachet with Her Back Turned*, *Warriors from the Yang Family*, and *Zhong Wuyan.* At noon, I glued the radio on my ear, listening to Lee Ngo's Sky Novel or Tang Kee Chan's sitcoms (where the dramatist performed a wide range of five or six character voices in an episode). In the evening, I enjoyed Cantonese operas such as *Liang Wudi: An Emperor-Turned-Monk* and *The Monk Praying for the Soul of His Deceased Lover.* Although those live performances were widely popular, and easily got re-played a dozen times, I always missed the last couple of scenes in each opera, as Mother never allowed me to stay up past my bedtime.

Local radio programs became more entertaining after Rediffusion introduced its service in Hong Kong. Because there were many choices to choose from, Mother began to impose curfews on me lest I would go overboard. Naturally, speaking of content diversity, there was just no comparison between olden days and now. Nevertheless, we lived in an era where there were no illusions or pretensions. The broadcaster did an honest day's work by telling a story; the listener truly enjoyed it. And everybody was happy. While Chan Gung delivered his version of *Water Margin*, and Yip Ci Hong gave his own interpretation of *Romance of the Three Kingdoms*, they also threw in a smattering of knowledge about history, literature, and phonemics. Fong Wing's versions of great stories, such as *A Biography of Jigong* and *Seven Heroes and Five Gallants*, never ended. He customarily touched on principles for proper conduct that always concluded with: "Everything in the universe embodies the Law of Cause and Effect." Apart from those all-time favorite stories, contemporary works such as *Sunrise*, *Thunderstorm*, *The Family*, and *Southward Bound* were also adapted for radio.

I had not known that I was geographically so close to the Mainland until I tuned in on To To's Biography of Ha Kau. Only then did I learn that it lies right behind Lion Rock in the Kowloon Peninsula. My heart was jumping with joy the whole day! Later on, there were Chung Wai Ming's *Lin Shirong*, and *Fang Shiyu*, which were mainly kung-fu stories, but to a certain extent they revolved around teachings such as "endure humiliation before you achieve your goal", "protect the weak and curb the violent", and "praise the good and condemn the bad".

Maybe, the broadcasters were not as "cute", "flamboyant", and "friendly" (or "out of line" — it depends on where you stand) as today's big-name radio personalities. Yet, they knew how to carry themselves and keep their chin up in adversity. Their voices may have long been forgotten by most people, but I am grateful to them for filling my childhood years with their stories. There is a perpetual aura around each of them that will always stay close to my heart.

June 20, 1980

Street Scenes

Before the advent of television, I watched what was happening in the neighborhood to pass the time in my early life.

But there was not much to watch. In point of fact, it was not a vibrant section of Hennessy Road that was lined with shops. Across the street from my childhood home, there were a grocery shop, a tailor's shop, a bakery, a rice merchant's shop, and three Chinese herbal medicine shops. They mainly served the population within the district. Their signboards, did not give me any clue how long they had been in business, had a timeless quality as if they had been hung outdoors forever. In those days, it was rather unusual for shop owners to place an ad in the newspaper. However, customers had a good head for figures. Which shop offered fair and square prices, and which shop did not, they all knew it like the back of their hand.

Compared to other shops, the restaurant with a magnificent sea-life mural was like a breath of fresh air. It had earned the affectionate nickname "Weird Fish" from kids in the neighborhood. Why was that? Nobody asked the question. Each year, before it was closed over the Chinese New Year break, a guy showed up to paint a new picture on the exterior wall. While the design was different from year to year, the subjects depicted in it remained unchanged. They were a mermaid and a scuba diver wearing a helmet. We kids all considered it a big annual event. While we watched the guy paint, our mind was working furiously: What kind of pose does the mermaid strike this year? How many weird fish will there be? The fresh paint on the mural heralded a new year. It was such a joyful sight that we actually oohed and ahhed at it every day until the paint layers weathered, and the color faded without our noticing. At that point, the year would almost come to its end.

In the evening on a normal day, Weird Fish lit up. All the bright joy of a happy occasion was magnified, completely at variance with the long street which remained incredibly quiet. A troupe of Cantonese opera singers was usually invited by the host to give a performance. Firecrackers were commonly used before the banquet began. We did not enjoy such a display because of the pungent choking smell of smoke in the air and the excessive amount of noise it produced on an undisturbed evening, but we watched it with interest just the same. As a matter of fact, the length of a roll of firecrackers reflected the host's wealth. When the display was over, some kids went through a mountain of torn pieces of paper tubes, fighting over little firecrackers that had not been exploded. There was plenty of excitement in the evening street when the air still smelled strongly of lingering smoke.

During the day, foot traffic was not high either. However, every now and then, something unusual happened. When a funeral procession was coming down the street, it created a buzz among kids. We did not understand death and did not grief ourselves, but something told us it was not supposed to be a joyous occasion. With a somber expression, we watched without saying a word when the procession passed. It was led by a pair of white lanterns with blue characters, a group of musicians playing Chinese and Western musical instruments while marching in a not-too-perfect formation, a sedan chair covered with white curtains inside which the coffin hid, and finally the family members of the deceased, wearing mourning attire and holding each other close. Silently, we listened to the blare of trombones, the beat of drums, and (occasionally) the wail of a grieving family member. All the time our ears were burning, our hearts throbbing. When the crowd of onlookers dispersed, the long street was its old self again.

June 27, 1980

Coal and Wood

More often than not, I was reduced to tears when helping out in the smoke-filled kitchen.

Don't get me wrong! This isn't a woeful story about a child slave. It is about the use of coal and wood as a cooking fuel in the past. And I learned it at first hand.

When coal and wood starts to burn, the fire may seem fickle, but it gives off the densest smoke. It is particularly hard to light a fire with wet wood, and you also need to pay attention to detail when arranging coals and small pieces of wood in layers. First, too much ash in the hearth is a problem. Clear it away. Get some yesterday's newspapers (which are easier to ignite), and screw them into loose balls. On top of the paper balls, stack up the coals and the wood alternately, such that a "raft" with plenty of space to allow air-flow is formed. Make sure that you choose a mixture of thick and thin and pile thick atop of thin. Now, the construction is there to support the fuel. It will burn merrily and sustain your fire. Use a hand-held fan to shoot air into the fire and accelerate the burning process, especially in the case of coal. However, there is some wrist technique for fanning the flames. If you use excessive force with the fan, you will only stir up dust from the bottom of the hearth rather than help the fire blaze nicely. I actually used a bamboo tube instead of a fan to serve the purpose. It was a hollow object about one foot long that my family called a "fire tube". I inserted one end of it into the hearth, pressed the other end against the mouth, and blew hard. The fire would start burning in no time.

However, even if you have mastered the techniques of layering the wood and fanning the flames, there is no guarantee that heavy smoke can be prevented. Heating efficiency of firewood depends on the density and moisture content of wood. You get low-quality firewood and smoke permeates the whole place. Fumes hanging heavily in the air definitely do not constitute a great picture to inspire poetry. They just make your eyes water. And it is not a pretty sight when it is time to prepare a meal and you have lit a fire in several wood-burning stoves. The modern generation cooks with kerosene, liquefied petroleum gas or gas. All that is a bit over their head.

Back then, there was one more task to carry out before anything else. It was wood splitting. Bigger chunks of firewood tended to be cheaper in price. They were delivered in a load by a shop assistant to our front door, and piled up in a hallway just outside the kitchen. Since a large block of wood was harder to catch fire than kindling, it was best to cut it into quarters. We had a maul and an ax at home. My parents used the big and heavy maul to hew a knotty block while I used the small and lightweight ax to split a branch. Sometimes my parents left their job unfinished, and I just completed it by breaking up a chunk down to the size I needed.

There is something reckless in splitting wood. An expert swings a maul one-handed in a wide arc right into a log held firm under the other hand on a chopping block. Instantaneously the log flies apart into two pieces of firewood. However, yours truly was a chicken-hearted softie. I never tried anything too risky. As always, I dutifully thrust the ax into the wood until it got wedged inside. Then, I pounded them on the chopping block a few times. Eventually it would split with a crack.

After the wood was split, firewood was to be stacked neatly in layers. And that was all in a day's work – yuppie! Really, I did not mind doing the chores, except that if I was not careful, a splinter would get lodged in the finger. Mother usually removed it with a simple needle and treated the minor cut with Merbromin. Of course, nothing serious would happen, but having the finger pierced by a splinter was unpleasant. I would not wish it on anybody.

July 7, 1980

Lessons Learned from Cantonese Films

People my age grew up watching black-and-white Cantonese films made in Hong Kong. Unknowingly, our views on different topics such as moral issues, value systems, and outlooks on life were more or less affected. Following the death of Mother, Father spent a big chunk of his pastime going to the cinema. Father and I seldom, if ever, missed a new film. Several decades later, I re-watched some of them. I must confess that they are thought-provoking. Before I forget, I will jot down some of the revelatory insights that they offer me.

About Law Enforcement in Imperial China

In the prototypical Cantonese historical drama film, law enforcement is in accord with the preferences of a minority group in Imperial China.

How so? The emperor and government officials (be they scrupulous or corrupt) all belong to a minority group. You scratch my back and I will scratch yours. Anything can be done easily by pulling a few strings. Nepotism is the handmaiden of the government. Whether it is a case where the court is connected directly to the emperor, or a panel of three judges presides over a notorious trial, or a plainclothes ombudsman investigates a complaint in the region, or Judge Bao (who cosplays as a ghost) extorts a confession from the suspect, the issue is not technical legality, it is the power of the court.

When the emperor/judge (be he scrupulous or corrupt) slams his wooden block onto the table for effect, both the plaintiff and the defendant are allowed to build a narrative for their cases. However, the good guy, for some reason, is usually wronged. The court orders that he be beaten with a large stick eighty times. He passes out, and is thrown into jail. Then the emperor/judge retires from the courtroom to consider his verdict. Surrounded by his team of legal advisors whose cunning eyes dart around everywhere, the emperor/judge lends his ear to their whispering words. A decision is made, which provides a blueprint for indictment. The court resumes next day, but the dice are loaded. The good guy is sent to the execution ground. Fortunately, a moment before an executioner brings down the cleaver, an eye-witness or a person with a clear conscience steps forward. In a few enlightening words, he/she manages to convince everyone. The emperor/judge inclines to right a wrong. In order to redress a grievance, he offers the good guy and/or his family member a position in the government. Sometimes he even goes the extra mile and arranges a marriage for the good guy's daughter or maid. Everybody is happy now. Thank you Your Majesty/My Lord! And the bad guy is condemned to death, or is exiled to Siberia. That is the end of the film.

In local films, the law is enforced by paddling, detention and imprisonment, and capital punishment. The emperor, a judge, a legal advisor, sometimes a senior official's madam, or even an ambitious empress dowager who rules the country behind the curtain in the palace can investigate crimes and apprehend offenders if he/she likes. In this very simplistic model of law enforcement, only a handful of people – and no one else – are in charge.

About Storytelling on Local Film

In a nutshell, the story moves forward too slowly at the beginning of the film, but picks up speed toward the end.

Generally, narrative events may be related in linear order, in medias res, or by the way of taking the narrative back in time from the current point in the story. In most of the black-and-white Cantonese films, the linear narrative technique is extensively used. Occasionally special effects are produced to show that the scene is a flashback, like, the edges of the picture are deliberately blurred. And there is a simple formula for unfolding a story. The opening pace always feels too slow, drastically different from that of the last fifteen minutes of the story. Since there is plenty of time left in the first- and second-third of the film, the story must contain a great deal of detail. Scenes are to be unhurriedly established. The same thing with or without additional embellishment is repeated over and over again by different persons. Living people talk, talk, and talk. Dying people talk, gasp for breath, and talk, imparting important information before they draw the last breath, cock the head to one side, and die. Sometimes even a ghost appears in a dream and talks. In the old days, the audience listened dutifully, despite the fact that everything was crystal clear.

However, there is still time left. So, the narrative pace has to slow down even further. The leading actor must not know the truth. He has to be kept in the dark. The leading lady, who has been wronged, must zip her lips. There is usually a close-up shot to show her face. Without fail, she sheds a single tear, but it takes forever for the tear to run down her cheek. "I was forced into prostitution, but I can't tell you why. Not now. You'll know why eventually. I'm doing this for you," she says sorrowfully in a halting voice. This made the audience grit their teeth. How they wished they appeared on the big screen, and redressed the situation!

That said, every so often local films employ in medias res to bypass superfluous exposition. Most commonly, this is through a normal cut to a wide shot of a flowing river onto which flower petals fall, or a tree on which flowers open and wither. During that time, the protagonist has reached adulthood, or has grown into old age. Additionally, a text message of "eighteen years later" appears to indicate time passing. It is a technique to signal the cinematic passage of time, skipping unimportant events, excluding any details of those years that are not vital to the story, and alerting the audience to events that have yet to take place in the process of narration.

Then in the last five to fifteen minutes of the film, the pace is upped. Rapid sequencing puts a spring into the narrative's step. Nobody prattles on. Everybody is concise in speaking and says much in few words. Suddenly, the protagonist becomes sharp-minded and quick-thinking. The bad guy repents of his evil-doings when his conscience at last catches up with him. "I've made a mistake and it's my fault. Please forgive me, I've done you wrong!" All grievances are now water under bridge. Oh, how wonderful! There is always a blue sky after the rain!

Such a formula for telling a story may not have a disadvantage. Since audiences are frustrated, they all heave a sigh of relief when the pace picks up toward the end. The climax is approaching. The film draws to a close. "Thank goodness, it's over!" Phew!

About Cantonese Film Audiences

Back then, audiences knew where they stood with local films. They were passive onlookers who were omniscient but could not intervene. They were auto-masochists who were all-wise but acted stupid.

Since I myself was an avid consumer of local film, I have a conflict of interest here. Still, I will try to conduct an objective analysis of the old-day film audience as best as I can.

Because of the narrative style to which local films conformed, we, as an audience, were all-knowing, even though the screenplay writer threw mists before our eyes. Behind a curtain, the silhouette of a leading lady looks like a ghost. Her black robe is flapping – now you see me, now you don't. Yet we knew that she was human, for a screenplay writer in those days would never influence popular beliefs about imaginary ghosts. Moreover, we were a pretty good judge of character. It was because Pak Yin, Nan Hong, Ka Ling, Chan Po Chu, Josephine Siao, Cheung Wood Yau, Wu Chu Fan, Wu Fung, Tse Yin, and Lui Kei were all "good-guy" actors and actresses. They never portrayed villains. But if they did, the bad guy in the film has to be a twin or an imposter. On the contrary, To Sam Ku, Lau Hak Suen, Chau Chi Sheng, Billy Fung, and Lam Mui Mui never took the role of a "good guy", although in a film they may be all smiles, uttering sweet words from the mouth.

As the story goes on, the main character has been wronged. A dishonest man is wagging his poisonous tongue. The lead is being threatened by a thug. The bad guy holds a handgun or knife, his Ascot cap askew, the short tunic of his kung-fu suit unbuttoned, and a cigarette dangling from his mouth. The lead is always incapable of making his/her escape. He/she keeps running into a table corner, and hurts himself/herself again and again while the thug is chasing him/her around a coffee table. As an audience, we were on pins and needles, both anxious and frustrated at once. We wished we were there to spill the beans or offer a helping hand. But then we remembered abruptly that we were just onlookers. There was nothing we could do about it. My, it was such an all-encompassing feeling of helplessness!

What I have mentioned above gives a reason why I consider the local-film audience all-wise. As to why I consider the audience stupid, it is helpful to think of it in two ways. From the perspective of a screenplay writer/director, we were slow on the uptake. In order to get a message across, things had to be repeated over and over again. He painstakingly dotted the i's and crossed the t's until we uttered aloud: Oooh, I see! From the perspective of viewers, we only had ourselves to blame. We bought a ticket and entered the cinema voluntarily, where we threw ourselves at the mercy of a screenplay writer/director. We felt helpless. We allowed ourselves to be tortured by anxious thoughts. Weren't we the dumbest persons in the world?

About Human Relationships

Black-and-white Cantonese films ascertain the boundary between good and evil. They are full of perceptive insights into the premise of the ultimate triumph of good and defeat of evil. They teach the truth that you reap what you sow.

Since actors and actresses in the past always played the same kind of role in multiple films, their iconic image of a good/bad guy simply stayed in our mind. Once in a while To Sam Ku portrayed a kind-hearted landlady in a film, we became suspicious. We were kept on the edge of our seats right through to the end. And when Pak Yin, for one time only, accepted the role as a murderous femme fatal who is capable of poisoning a foe, our feelings were hurt when we left the cinema.

The good and evil dichotomy had a beneficial influence on us as a whole.

Firstly, there was no need to live life being afraid of our shadow. It was a comforting thought to accept that people were either good or bad, contrary to the popular belief in recent years that human nature is complex — "Your worst enemy could be your best friend, and your best friend your worst enemy." We always asked an adult before a film started, "Is this person a good guy or bad guy?" Once the answer was clear, we immediately knew which side to take.

Secondly, we were taught from a young age to fully expect that morality was absolute. For that reason, no kid was willing to portray a villain in a role-playing game. Naturally, this type of thinking has translated into the unwritten law: good is rewarded with good, and evil with evil. We strongly believe that what goes around comes around. We are able to endure hardship, the reason being that we have high hopes for the future. We do not panic even if we depart this world before we taste anything sweet. We trust that after our death, we will be born again as a different person. Or we will turn into butterflies dancing among flowers, or flying toward a rainbow in the sky. There is eternal life in heaven. There is a happy ending. What happens to the bad guy? It goes without saying that punishment awaits him/her.

Local films give us this type of moral education, and we find it beneficial to a child's development. We have strong moral ideas, stick to our principles, and are willing to wait patiently for a reward. However, human nature has undergone qualitative changes in recent years. Some people taking a more realistic, multi-dimensional approach suggest that an individual is capable of both good and evil. If easy notions of "good guys" and "bad guys" are challenged, and even the principle of "sowing and reaping" is compromised, we people grew up watching local films will have a hard time in building a social life. There is not a lot to hang our hat on. Fortunately, before we know it, the deaths of Ceausescu and his wife in Romania prove that we have been right. Now our self-confidence is boosted. Life goes on as usual because there is hope dangling in front of us.

March 26, 1990

At the Entrance to The Mandarin

Like the memories of my younger years, the landscape outside of a window gets misty if the glass fogs up. Only when the wind dies down and condensation goes away is the entire scene in sharp focus.

***

It's Saturday noontime. I station myself at the entrance to a multi-story colonial building in Central on Hong Kong Island. The balconies hang out over the sidewalk.

The sun is shining bright. It's one of those Saturdays that make me happy. The Star Ferry Pier is located right across the street not far away from where I am standing. In a few minutes, Father will stride out of the pier. His kung-fu suit makes him stand out from the rest of commuters. Most of them wear a suit. The street that runs between the colonial building and the waterfront is too narrow to be obstructive. Occasionally a couple of cars speed by, but that doesn't ruin my chance to spot Father leaving the pier. That said, the frequency of ferries is pretty low. If he misses his ferry, I don't see why I can't have a little fun.

Let me skip over to a parking lot next to the colonial building, and take a quick look at those compact economy cars. I start counting them up. There are black cars and gray cars, all elegant and in pristine condition under the blazing sun. I love small cars. This is the only place where I can find so many of them. After a while, I return to the sidewalk outside the colonial building. Still, I don't see any ferry draw near the pier.

I look upward. The massive concrete columns that hold up the colonial building are covered in grayish-white dust, and appear almost charcoal in color. They stand real high, towering over me. Although I take refuge under the balconies, the pier bathed in the bright sun makes me squint.

I know it. The moment Father emerges from the pier, he'll instinctively glance up at the third floor of the colonial building. It's where the island branch of the Whampoo Dock Company Limited is located. Father is in the Company's employ but doesn't go to work there. He works in the Kowloon office. I don't know anything about this branch office on the third floor, except that a signboard hangs from the external wall. A big English word with five letters is written on it[1]. I recognize all the letters. Still and all, I haven't the slightest idea how to pronounce that word. Once I asked Father but got no answer from him. Since he works in a dockyard owned by Europeans, he must be fluent in English. Yet, I've never heard him speak in that language.

Father knows everything. He told me it's the signboard of a renowned European travel agency that opened its first branch office in Shanghai. But I don't know what the word travel means. "It means that someone goes on a cruise or takes a plane to visit all places around the world. Those places are far, far away," he said. I don't want to go to places far, far away. How far is far? I don't know. Every day he takes a ferry to cross the harbor and goes to work in Kowloon. That's far away, I suppose. "You're only eight, just a kid. When you turn eighteen, your mother and I will bring you along to go on a trip around the world. And Tung Chai Lung Travel will make arrangements for us. It's the Chinese name of the European travel agency[2] on the third floor," he said. I've read *Kwong Cheung Lung: The Haunted Inn*, but I've never heard Tung Chai Lung, the travel agency. For that reason, I always associate the travel agency with a haunted inn. I don't think about traveling, for I have to go a long time before I turn eighteen. And I still haven't figured out what travel means. Once I asked Mother if we'd go traveling one day. "Yes, we'll take a trip to the Mainland if we have enough money. But we won't go on a trip around the world," she replied. "Will Tung Chai Lung Travel make arrangements for us?" I asked. "No, it won't. It specializes in around-the-world tours," she said. I didn't pursue the question, as I had already lost interest in the subject.

---

[1] Translator's note: It was Cook's.

[2] Translator's note: It was Thomas Cook and Son.

Now, I'm still waiting for Father to walk onto the street. I guess he has missed his ferry. When he arrives, we'll head west along the harbor front out of force of habit. We'll pass by a row of high-rises, low-rises, and the office of the Secretariat for Chinese Affairs that faces the Vehicular Ferry Pier across the street. Then we'll turn into the main street where the tram runs services. Ordinarily, Father lingers in front of Pak Doy, an electrical appliances shop, peering into the windows where a collection of machines is on display. But, as usual, I want to get a move on, tugging at his sleeve, and urging him forward. Chung Kwok, the upstairs dim sum restaurant next to Sincere (a department store) is always packed to maximum capacity when it's near one o'clock. However, we never have to wait for a table, as we can rely on Uncle Tim to reserve one for us. Uncle Tim serves dim sum in the restaurant. He is an old-timer and we're buddies.

It's a happy Saturday. I'm waiting for Father in the entranceway of a colonial building in Central. We're going to have dim sum. Where's he?

***

The Star Ferry Pier across the street glows. It glows in the sunlight and glares. It seems to move away from me as I hear the bell in a secular tower chime. A steady stream of vehicles blocks my view into the street.

I tilt my head and see light reflected from huge glass doors. I am standing at the front doors to The Mandarin.[3] [4]

April 20, 1988

[3] Translator's note: The Mandarin was built on the former site of the colonial Queen's Building.

[4] Author's note: A documentary about Hong Kong has inspired me to write this essay.

The Love of a Father

In my works, I often talk about Mother but seldom speak of Father. My friends always wonder if I had resented Father and the two of us had a falling-out. In point of fact, the reality was quite different.

After I read Wang Zengqi's essay in *Paternal Love* edited by Gu Jian, the penny dropped. Only then did I realize that my father had loved me like a brother.

Mother was a strict disciplinarian. She ensured that my mind was directed to do appropriate things. Father was equally opposite in strictness. He was full of fun. But in Mother's words, he was "roguish" and a "bad example to kids". He was a prankster. And there was no way to know if he was pulling my leg. Once Mother told me a story of how three military men in Ancient China — Liu Bei, Guan Yu, and Zhang Fei — had their fraternal relationship sealed in a solemn initiation ceremony under a peach tree. He overheard her account. Later that day, Father and I went window-shopping. He related to me a small anecdote about the three guys. Liu, Guan, and Zhang were made by God out of flour. One by one they were left in an oven to bake. Unfortunately, God was not quite diligent in checking on them for doneness. In consequence, they had pale, ruddy, and dark skin respectively.

When he took me for a walk around the streets in Sai Ying Pun, he recounted many a fascinating story about prostitutes soliciting customers in the Island's oldest red-light district. Just like anyone else, he had been young and wild. My parents browsed through several newspapers every day. Mother followed closely international development news, whereas Father enjoyed reading sensational news stories on diverse subjects. To sustain his unorthodox interests, I was required to create scrapbooks with all those newspaper clippings that he found entertaining. While Mother expected me to memorize the names of the one hundred and eight heroes as recorded in the classic novel The Water Margin, Father taught me the set of thirty-six names used in the zihua gambling game.

Because he was full of pep, he wanted me to play games for boys, like, lion dancing, drumming, swordsmanship, and northern-style martial arts. I had learned a few drum beats and a few steps of the lion dance because of him. Once, Father and I practiced sword fighting on the balcony. As I started at step one, thrusting my toy sword up above the head, I broke the glass shade of a ceiling lamp.

Nothing worried Father, he was really laid back. After Mother was gone, he allowed me to invite classmates over, and accepted them readily as his friends. Father and I almost never missed a movie playing in the National Cinema and the Universal Cinema. We walked every street and left our footprints all over the city. He was the one who provided me with valuable information on humanitarian ideals and liberal arts. There is no doubt about it.

However, unlike Wang, I had a very different upbringing. Father was not committed to my education. When I was finishing grade six, I asked for his advice. "It's pretty much your call," he simply said. It was his way to raise a kid. To this day, I can close my eyes and remember that mischievous grin on his face.

February 15, 2009

Going to the Cantonese Opera

Over the weekend, I read in the newspaper that watching Cantonese movies and going to the Cantonese opera used to be the two most common leisure activities in the British colony. Most people my age recall that in our childhood whenever mum (or mum's sister, or dad's sister) went to the theater, we tagged along. My case was different. Mother was an avid reader, Cantonese operas, or should I say all kinds of musical plays, did not float her boat. Moreover, she dreaded to think that my academic scores would drop if I spent too much time watching operas. To make sure that it did not happen, she set a strict limit on the amount of time I could spend on going to the opera. However, Father was a big opera fan. He almost never missed a performance delivered in the theater. And I was a Daddy's girl. Every time an opera premiered, he would convince Mother to relax my opera time limits.

The drum beat. The gong banged. The opera story did not interest me as much as actors' and actresses' agile movements on stage and flashy costumes in bright red and green. I committed to memory every dramatic gesticulation that caught my eye and every simple expression that was easy enough to roll off the tongue. Later at home, Father and I did role plays. But when things were a little out of hand, we got ourselves into trouble. Mother would be mad as hell. One year, Father bought me a pair of metal toy swords from the Lunar New Year bazaar. We then had a sword fight on the balcony. I raised the sword high up in the air, and the next thing I knew I broke the shade of a ceiling lamp. On another occasion, Father assumed the imaginative role of a jockey. He showed me how to use a whip in horse racing, but swept a glass-lined vacuum flask off the table instead.

Still and all, I was also an enthusiast for more "civilized" games. Father was the partner I practiced sword fighting with. When he was at work, I inserted my arms into the long, wide pant legs of his kung-fu suit, and performed a sleeve dance. Like a professional, I whirled my "water sleeves" around, flicking them again and again.

Father's responses to my curious questions concerning opera always mingled truth with falsehood. If Mother found out, she would bluntly tell him to act his age. Like, Father and I went to see the production of *The Lord of Six States.* I noticed that several actors who wore a trash can on their heads hollered WO-HO when they entered the stage. Father told me they were extras. I did not understand why the bearded actor in a prop vehicle (I did not know that he played the role of Gongsun Yan) kept pacing the floor. Father explained that the guy was agitated, because Su Qin was appointed chief administrator but forgot to gift him *lai see* money. I was completely baffled by the maid's behavior. When the protagonist rose to his feet, she lifted a chair off the floor, and brought it back down with a hard thud. Father told me that she was really pissed off moving chairs and tables around all the time.

Those were some of the things I learned from Father. Fortunately, I had a habit of parroting back information to Mother. She was the one who straightened me out on a lot of things on the subject of tradition and culture.

March 13, 2010

Mother's Version of the Story

My parents differed radically from one another in their ways to raise a kid. To take an example, their responses to my questions concerning opera were as different as chalk and cheese. When I asked questions about *The Lord of Six States*, Mother set out with a lecture on Chinese tradition and culture.

"During the Spring and Autumn Period and the Warring States Period, when people from a respectable family introduced themselves, they gave their names, birthplaces, and official ranks to impress others, like, 'I'm Lord Wen from the state of Yan.' Art imitates life. Extras in the background are part of the scene. They appear in a non-speaking capacity. When they enter the stage, they merely cry out wo-ho, as in mat-gam wo-ho, an expression we use in Cantonese to show disapproval of the behavior of a loser. Mind you, the leading character in The Lord of Six States isn't Su Qin. It's Gongsun Yan. He forges an alliance between the six states in his capacity as a representative."

"Why did the actor keep pacing the floor on stage?" I asked.

"Imagine that he was operating a vehicle. He was moving from one place to another. While he was 'driving', he was given an opportunity to show off his agility and body techniques by tossing his long beard and making quick movements of the waist and legs. Besides, cultural etiquette in Ancient China dictated that a guest kept turning around to bow to his host as he took his leave. And a host didn't close the door until his guest was far down the road. It has nothing to do with lai see money. Proper codes of behavior are a concern."

Apparently Father was a realist. His cooked-up stories made me bark up the wrong tree. (Nowadays, I notice that older people still conform to this rule of etiquette required of a polite host. The host stays standing in the door while the guest keeps bowing after he or she is escorted out.

The same rule of courtesy is adopted in Japan. There is a French cartoon that depicts a Japanese host looking through a telescope in the direction of his retreating guest while both parties keep bowing deeply to each other.)

"Why did a maid lift a chair and bang it down hard?" I asked.

"It was a signal to caution that the chair had been pulled out so as to avoid a fall-down accident," Mother replied.

I listened dutifully. (Since then, I have made a mental note to whisper a word of caution whenever I need to pull out a chair for someone.)

"Likewise, if something brittle is to be passed from hand to hand, it's always useful to let the recipient know before withdrawing your hand from it. Sometimes people just miscalculate their timing, and the object is dropped to the floor. There's no point in crying over spilled milk, is there?" Mother added.

She had led me down a path strewn with those wisest truths she made part of my daily life.

March 14, 2010

Ever-White Mountain, Here I Come!

I arrived in Ever-White Mountain — some fifty years late.

Everything began when Mother was confined to bed by her last illness for three years. While the cause of her illness remained unknown, her health was deteriorating. She was treated by both physicians and Traditional Chinese Medicine practitioners but all to no avail. She developed photophobia and was acutely sensitive to cold air. During that time, not much light was admitted into our house. All of the windows were kept closed. The curtains were drawn. The whole family was locked in, not unlike the Zhous depicted in *Thunderstorm*.

After school, I stayed at Mother's bedside, listening to her feeble voice recounting mythological stories from China and other parts of the world. Occasionally, I took her to the doctor's office. It was a stressful experience for a twelve-year-old kid. More than once, she collapsed in the street before we reached the clinic. One time, her Traditional Chinese Medicine practitioner, Cheung Bak Sheung, suggested that she take ginseng grown in the Ever-White Mountain territories as a natural remedy. That was the first time the name of the mountain popped up. Mother dismissed the idea because it was too costly. Later at home, I asked her about the remedy. She patiently told me stories about the herb, the Mountain, the Black Dragon River, and even the Japanese invasion of Northeast China. From that time on, I made it my business to go to the Mainland to get ginseng for my sick mother.

She never had a chance to taste it. Three years later, she died after an operation at Queen Mary Hospital.

There were always places in Hong Kong to buy top-grade Ever-White Mountain ginseng, but by the time I could afford it, Mother was long gone. I promised myself I would make that trip regardless.

It was not as easy as I thought it would be, though. To begin with, I needed to round up enough people to form a tour group. And when the mountain became a popular tourist attraction, I held my horses. I was not really fit to go hiking. The last thing I wanted was to spoil the trip for everyone else in the group. But after careful consideration, I thought the issue was not my health condition. It was now or never.

So, I made it to the Mountain! I crawled up the northern, western, and southern slopes, and made an inspection of the area. Sadly, ginseng farms were nowhere to be found. Ginseng, the "king of herbs and medicines", was only sold in tourist gift shops.

I was as good as my word, except that I returned home empty-handed from my trip.

October 25, 2008

Reminiscences of the Past

My sixty-five-year-old sister and sixty-six-year-old cousin are in the sitting room of my flat. Over the past four hours, they have been chattering away about almost everything under the sun, from childhood memories to recent births and deaths of family members and acquaintances, from the ups and downs of life to the love-hate struggle between man and woman. Every now and then their high-pitched voices are toned down to compensate for news about a mishap or a stroke of bad luck.

I have seated myself between them.

My cousin had been out of touch with my sister and me for decades. Now the two of them are telling me things that sound like a movie. In the movie, I am surprised to discover many camera shots of me going through different development stages.

I was a newborn infant.

I was walking unassisted with feet wide apart and arms held high to maintain balance.

I tagged along with my sister to class when I started school. I got lessons from my cousin and learned to count to ten.

One after another, a distinct yet blurred image of my former self has taken shape. It gets sharpened in some way by their disjointed fragments of information. Everything is both real and unreal. Although I know they are talking about me, it is almost as if they were talking about someone else, or about a life before this one I am living currently.

Maybe it is rather unusual for someone my age to listen to older people's tittle-tattling about things of a bygone era. While their idle talk evokes memories that have started to fade, I am trying frantically to figure out what actually happened. But it is a futile attempt to re-construct a time long lost. My sis and cousin change the subject so fast that my head spins. It is too hard to keep up with them.

"You loved going out. You wouldn't stop bawling until I got you out of the house. Father doted on you. He made it clear that I should put family before homework. The moment you started crying, I had to drop everything and to give you a piggyback ride in the street. You were a spoilt brat!"

"You couldn't write the number 8 correctly. You just drew two circles like a snowman, so your teacher made you write it down a hundred times as punishment. I was super-patient with you. Still, you couldn't produce a fluid 8 and you kept crying. You were such a noodle!"

All those harsh words that once made me flinch have softened now. They sound affectionate to my ear. I am forming a mental image of a noodle and spoilt brat blessed with a jovial childhood! Was that really me? And how many more times will I listen to their stories?

With little warning, I feel a wave of emotion come over me.

December 21, 1992

A Candy Craving

Suddenly, I crave for a hard milk candy.

Is there any problem? I hear you ask! Yes, there is. The popular brand of candy from when I was a kid no longer exists.

I knew nothing of its brand name and place of origin. However, I do remember that it came in a round tin container on which there was a picture of a glass of milk. Each candy was wrapped up in a slip of red, white, and blue glossy wax paper. Several English words were printed on the wrapper, but they meant nothing to me.

The product was imported from overseas. It was a real treat during Lunar New Year, as my family could not afford it on ordinary days. But even so, Mother would dole out more than half of the candies to friends and relatives. And she rationed the rest. Once every few days, she gave me a couple of candies, and left me facing the dilemma of chowing them down all at once or saving one for school recess the next day. Usually I would go with the latter. All good things were worth waiting for. I simply could not bear the thought of stuffing all of them in my mouth at one go.

The moment I sucked on a candy, a pleasantly sweet, milk-flavored, and satiny-smooth taste began to make a gentle path down the throat. I smoothed out the slip of confectionery paper with my hands as flat as I could. I folded it in half, and, voilà, it became my "treasure". While all other kids preferred the colorful aluminum foil paper for wrapping chocolate, I loved the simple and clean design of the wax paper. It took ten of them to make one bookmark, which was more durable than that made of aluminum foil wrappers. Toying with my bookmark that was different from the others', I could not help but yearn for the coming of the next new year. The taste of my childhood was as sweet as the milk candy in the mouth.

Now I can eat as many milk candies as I want, but that particular brand is no longer unavailable. I feel lost. However, I think everything works out for the best in the end. What if that brand of candy is brought back but tastes different? What if my sense of taste changes? After all, taste perpetually bound with memory can only mature over time.

I have a craving for a milk candy. But I would do better to give it a pass even if one was within reach.

May 22, 1983

Afternoon Tea

Why do I love afternoon tea?

Personally I do not use the word afternoon in its precise sense. The way I see it, it is a kind of reward for an honest half-day's work. It is a gap in a busy schedule, where I meet up with new friends, old friends (who share — or do not share — the same interests), casual acquaintances, former students, or current students (who tend to shift uncomfortably in their chairs and stare down into their cups) for an hour or two in a little cozy café or in a swanky hotel's coffee lounge crowded with holiday-makers. There is no agenda. There is no planned topic of conversation. Our conversation may be desultory, going from one subject to another, or even disconnected as to topics. But so what? We are with each other. We just chit-chat about this and that while an hour rolls away.

Usually I order a black tea with cream. I love the aroma of coffee, but do not really like the taste of it. So, it is just perfect if my companion sitting across from me sips at a cup of coffee. The smell of it is as pleasing as soft background music. I also need a generous slice of light cheesecake to complete my deluxe afternoon-tea set.

That said, it is equally acceptable to stay in my own room. I lounge in a comfortable chair. I drink slowly a cup of tea. I nibble on a cookie. I cast an occasional glance at passers-by through the window. I listen to the muffled sounds of the city's traffic and my feathered friends' songs. The racing thoughts in my mind become quiet.

In the seventies, the intense heat of the red sun was building up on the Mainland.

"You're such a bourgie!" A student of mine had a go at me when she found out that I often took a tea break in the afternoon.

I defended myself by asking her two questions. "Which social class people like cabinet-makers, plaster-workers, and house-painters belong to?"

"It's the working class."

My next question left her speechless. "They're entitled to a break at a quarter past three on a working day. What do you think?"

Is there anything wrong if we earn our keep and recharge our batteries with a little pampering? I have thought about it. It seems like it is the bourgeoisie's mentality, due to the assumption that only people in the city are financially comfortable enough to afford afternoon tea. However, on my visits to the countryside in Fujian and Szechuan, I learned that it was not unusual for peasants to take a break from work. They brought out a tea pot and cups. They plopped their butts down or relaxed in a bamboo chair, and started a conversation with friends.

A decent life allows us to indulge in moderate pleasures after hard work.

March 17, 1995

It's about Afternoon Tea Again

The indulgence in afternoon tea seems to run in my family.

In her time, Mother would have qualified as a traditional Chinese woman if she had not been a big fan of afternoon tea. She watched every penny to make ends meet. However, twice or thrice a month, she took her friends or Father and me to a nice coffee shop.

With like-minded friends, she usually went to the North Pole on Tin Lok Lane in Wan Chai District. The small café with a navy blue color scheme is well-remembered by old-timers. It was secluded and cozy. The interior walls were decorated with pictures of penguins standing on an iceberg. If it was a family day out, we usually went to Wiseman Restaurant or a coffee lounge on the ground floor of The Hong Kong Hotel. Occasionally we went to a coffee shop at The Cecil. All were located in Central.

What impressed me most was the one at the Hong Kong Hotel, where an entire wall of the coffee lounge was covered in glass. Sunlight entered through white sheer curtains that allowed for a flowing affect. I was dwarfed by the lofty ceiling and over-sized armchairs which surrounded a small glass-top coffee table. It certainly did not feel like fun to perch on the edge of the seat of an armchair thrice my size, my feet off the ground, my legs dangling, and my hands unable to reach the coffee table. Mother usually ordered a bottle of warm milk and a pot of black tea for herself. She prepared her own version of thé au lait without using the cream that came with the tea. There would also be a club sandwich more than an inch thick for the three of us to share. All kinds of ingredients were heaped together between two layers of bread separated by an additional slice. It was no easy task to take a bite of a sandwich that was much bigger than my mouth while using good table manners. No wonder the café left a deep impression on me.

After Mother passed away, Father did not break his habit of having afternoon tea. However, he stopped frequenting Wiseman Restaurant and The Hong Kong Hotel's coffee lounge altogether. Instead, he dropped by any café on his way to run errands. If he stayed home, he would go to Tai Ping Koon Restaurant in the neighborhood, or a small coffee shop next to the Golden City Cinema. The coffee shop was owned by a guy from Shanghai. Compared with Mother, Father was more willing to give me a free rein. When I was in grade six, he gave me permission to treat my buddies to a quick bite at the Shanghainese's coffee shop. The owner let me run a tab. Since Father was a loyal patron, he would pick up the bill on his next visit. At that time, a cup of milk tea cost seventy cents; a bottle of Green Spot, thirty cents; toast, fifty cents – take your pick, guys!

Ah, those were the days!

March 22, 1995

Snacks (I)

Former students of mine, most of them were my high-school students, bring me all kinds of snacks whenever they come visit me. I have no idea how they find out that I am a snack lover.

The Lunar New Year presents I have received include – let me estimate in my head – four kilograms of peanuts, close to twenty boxes of expensive candies and cookies, and different kinds of preserved fruits, prawn chips, and potato chips. They take up all the space in my kitchen pantry. I start to worry that they will go bad when the humidity level rises in spring. And I hate to see food wasted!

Well, if truth be told, I love to eat a small snack in between meals. It runs in the family. Father could not resist peanuts, preserved fruits, and pickled vegetables. After Mother was gone, nobody kept an eye on the two of us. We would easily munch our way through a few hundred grams of peanuts plus several bags of Hing Ah's preserved prunes and plums right after dinner while listening to the radio or vinyl records in the sitting room. Father was addicted to Cantonese-style snacks such as pickled vegetables, pickled sand pears, pickled papayas, pickled ginger, pickled bulbous onions, pickled Indian gooseberries, and pickled plums. There was a food vendor outside of the National Cinema. Whenever we went to watch a movie, we stopped at the stall to get a large bag of snacks. By the time the movie started, we had had everything wolfed down.

My former teacher, the late Mr. Zeng Keduan, was a snack lover too. There was a rich tapestry of seeds, jujube cakes, and preserved fruits in his northern-style candy box during Lunar New Year.

Retro snacks are different these days. Maybe, the quality of ingredients does matter. Or, recipes for old-time snacks (such as pickled sand pears and pickled papayas) have been lost. The making of snacks (such as preserved prunes and preserved plums) is not the same. Invariably, all snacks have a strange chemical taste that causes a sort of stinging sensation under the tongue. Deep-fried prawn chips and potato chips are heavily seasoned with MSG. None of them have a unique flavor. After a while, the palate gets bored with so much sameness.

Maybe, there has been a change in my appetite.

Or maybe, there has been a change in the way I look at things. I am the one who has changed. What I actually miss is one taste of the old time, like an early evening or a long, lazy summer afternoon, where neighbors dropped by for a chat. Peanut skins slipped off from the fingers, fluttering gently to the floor of the sitting room. The paper wrappers for preserved fruits were wadded up in the hand, making a faint crumpling sound.

March 26, 1995

Snacks (II)

I have inherited the habit of munching on snacks from Father.

Mother was a highly organized person who lived an austere life. She did not eat between meals, although every now and then she had a cup of hot coffee with milk and a sandwich in the afternoon. By contrast, Father was a big snack fan. We had only just finished dinner, and already he was talking about a bedtime snack, like, mung-bean sweet soup, red-bean sweet soup, tofu-skin sweet soup with ginkgo nuts and hard-boiled egg, almond sweet soup, or black-sesame sweet soup. And we never ate the same snack two days in a row.

When he was in the right mood, he would send me to a street stall on Thomson Road even if it was in the middle of a freezing winter evening. And off I went, carrying an aluminum cooking pot that served as a container, to get fish-ball noodle soup and boiled vegetables with oyster sauce. In addition to his bedtime snack, he stuffed himself with peanuts, preserved prunes, preserved plums, and salted olives while reading newspapers after dinner. That was his daily evening routine.

If he was going to watch a movie, food stalls at the entrance to the Universal Cinema or the National Cinema offered him a wide variety of treats such as pickled vegetables, pickled Daikon, pickled papayas, pickled sand pears, and coconut slices with pickled ginger. All of them he enjoyed immensely. When the chilly wind blew in winter, he bought a bag of warm, delicious-smelling roasted chestnuts and sweet potatoes, hugging it close to his chest as he went into the cinema. However, for some reason he never touched a morsel of aromatic roasted squid. And he did not like sweets, imported sweets in particular. For all I knew, confectionery from foreign countries did not come cheap. In my family, hard milk candies, chewy Sugus candies, and chocolates were the ultimate treat only during Lunar New Year.

When Father died, I did not have extra money to spend however I wanted. Throughout my high-school days, only peanuts were affordable.

Nevertheless, too much fiber subsequently caused digestive problems. It was then that I promised myself that when I started working, I would have the wall cabinets of my house lined with jars filled with goodies. Old friends and former students of mine have seen the gigantic jar of colorful chocolate beans in my sitting room. They will not forget the candy box that contains lots of treats I offer to guests during Lunar New Year.

Now I have enough money to buy whatever I want, I seldom let snacks pass my lips. I surely miss my childhood eats, but retro snacks are loaded with chemicals these days. They always leave a bitter taste in the mouth — or is that just me? Throwback candies are a bit sweet to my palate. Flavored peanuts come in many varieties, but they are packed full of additives. They seem to squeak against the teeth.

Ugh, that's life.

February 23, 2008

Part II

An apricot branch with pink flowers
Peeks out from a courtyard garden.
— Ye Shaoweng

Metamorphosis

Countable were days in the previous year, but uncountable were experiences I had gained in a foreign country. After I decided to take a step out of my comfort zone, I quit my job. When I gave my friends the heads-up that I would be away for a year, one frowned and considered it a luxury. Another chirped, "Cool!" I held my peace, and answered nothing. In a sense, they were both right.

It was so easy to fall into the trap of complacency in this city. Enthusiasm that once protected me like a knight's armor had rusted away. It was badly in need of repair. Maybe, a Hercules who was empowered by faith could be exempted from this consequence, but I was not one. Anyway, I liked the idea of leading my spirit to peace and sweet rest where I could do some deep soul searching. I hoped I would come back like a brand-new person. I set my sights on Kyoto, Japan and plunged in.

The choice was made based on three reasons. Firstly, I had given Professor Zuo Shunsheng my word of honor that I would go on a study trip to Japan. My book, *The Shadow Cast by the Sun*, published three years ago after a flying visit to this country was written at a very superficial level. I had every intention of having my curiosity sated. Secondly, I had ruled out countries like the United States, Canada, England, and France due to my low English proficiency level. By contrast, living in Japan might not be fraught with difficulty, as the people makes extensive use of Chinese characters. Thirdly, I was ready to return to Kyoto and spend a year there. It was a place I would never forget. While its air of timeless antiquity and elegant architectural styles of the Tang Dynasty absorbs an expert on the cultural commonalities between China and Japan, an eminence commanding a river or a pavilion surrounded by flowers and willows is sufficient to afford me a charming view of rural retirement of times long past. Besides, the library of Kyoto University houses a huge collection of Chinese books, where I could bury myself in publications pertaining to my research interests. I might not become more knowledgeable in a year's time, but at least I would live my dreams.

In dreams, time does not exist, as the saying goes. But outside of a castle in the air, one year had passed so fast. I felt like an infant girl whose face flushes with excitement when seeing fireworks for the first time in her life. However, as my hands reached out to the night sky, all sparkles and lights eluded me. I have composed my thoughts on my return from Japan. I have no plans to write up a self-appraisal, but I think I should fill my readers in.

Only now have I noticed that my first reason for choosing Kyoto was ridiculous. I was either being ignorant or having my head in the clouds when I believed that I would be able to learn more about a nation if I spent a year living in a single city and interacting with people in my circle of acquaintances! Where the two other reasons are concerned, I have to admit that I had been petty and spiteful. Having said that, I desire to write about the things I had seen, the people I had met, the books I had read, and the feelings I had had. Like reflections in mirrors or episodes of a documentary, they will serve to remind me of my stay in Japan.

To take a break from work and live off of my own savings is such a luxury. To follow my heart and live with abandon in a foreign country is real cool. But at the end of the day, did I manage to remove rust from my armor and to have it restored to a ship-shape appearance? To that question, I have no answer. But one thing is for sure: something inside of me has changed.

April 12, 1974

A Used-Book Store

Occasional flurries persisted through March in Kyoto. It was the best time to take a stroll around the city, as it was not cold enough to have to wear a winter hat. The sensation of feeling cool, soft flurries on the hair, the eyebrows, and the cheeks was indescribable. Snow is neither ice-cold nor stone-hard. Someone from the south probably finds it difficult to understand. Flakes of snow settled on the shoulders and the lapels of my coat. Before entering a house, I always paused under the awning to stomp my feet and brush the snow off my coat. Like tiny flower petals, little sprinkles of snow casually scattered over the ground as if they did not have a care in the world.

It was a typical day in March. I shook the free snow off my coat upon arrival at a modest used-book store in the late afternoon. The glass panel on the wooden door under a low awning was in need of a wash. It looked dusty enough to shield the shop interior from the public's prying eyes. If I got too close to it, the glass got foggy from my breath, obscuring whatever I saw inside. A left-hand entry door opened inward. But one had to watch out for the large wood doorsill, as I had seen a few patrons trip on it. The small shop was dimly lit, as if cigarette smoke had permeated it. Books took up all the space. At first glance, it seemed that heaps of Chinese and Japanese classics lay in disarray on the shelves. Upon closer examination, I noticed that they were kept organized by genre. Some of the larger box sets that included paperback volumes of classic texts were fastened with string. Some were bundled up in paper, on which book titles were written with a brush pen in bold, strong strokes. It was unlike today's dominant handwriting style that lacks vitality. Hung on a wall, a mechanical antique clock used a pendulum – tick-tock, tick-tock. The sound cut through the silence. I hesitated to pull out a book from the shelf or even to take a deep breath, lest the peace and quiet be shattered.

Only when I walked toward the rear of the shop did I become aware of two tatamis positioned next to an old fireplace. A svelte gentleman of advanced years wearing dark-colored, raw-textured traditional Japanese clothing sat seiza-style reading at a low table. More books were stacked up in a disorderly pile alongside. Was he the shop owner? He surely did not look like a book seller. Without lifting his gaze, he kept reading. He was all by himself in his own world. Oh well, live and let live. I browsed through some of his classy line of books, and found most of them unaffordable. I reckoned that only a scholarly bibliophile with money to burn was ready to pay for them. As I did not have two pennies to rub together, I was better off without making a purchase.

I whiled away an hour flipping through books until the sun faded away. The elderly shop owner rose to his feet. He turned on one dim light before returning his attention to the book that he had been reading. It was time to head home. I pushed the door open. Outside, the snow let up, but the temperature had dropped. By the time I paused and turned around, the shop, softly illuminated, was already in the distance.

December 25, 1976

My Faraway Country

The sun is closer;
Changan City is too far away.
— Liu Yiqing

Swathes of fine drizzle dampened a pathway, causing a thin mist veneer settling over the distance. I had visited Meiji-Jingu Shrine in a forest, where thirteen million trees of different species are grown. I had visited the torii that represents the apogee of Japanese design on postcards, which structurally resembles the Chinese character for a well and symbolically marks the transition from the mundane to the sacred. I had also visited the Imperial Palace, where Japanese tourists have their pictures taken at the main entrance with an air of solemnity and due reverence but Chinese tourists are arrogant and condescending — "Our Forbidden City is the real thing." As my shoes crunched on the gravel, I set off on my journey in Japan.

Lo and behold, I saw a rivulet quietly flow, fresh grass grow along the bank, weeping willows richly green, and a pair of delicate swallows with scissor-like tails cut straight into the wind… Everything was perfect like a dream. It had to be Jiangnan, a romantic vision of the region south of the lower reaches of the Yangtze River in China. I reached up and found several branches of willows hanging close overhead. But when I gently stroked them with my fingertips, my hand felt the damp chill of cold leaves. I shook myself out of my reverie to find a group of Japanese tourists standing beside me, listening attentively to a tour guide. All of a sudden, I felt an unusual twinge of pity for myself. I had never set foot in my own country. And here I was, hoping to catch a glimpse of her face in a foreign country. What a fool! I bit my lip, and recalled myself from such pathetic thinking with shame.

Nevertheless, I was capable of making the same mistake over and over. Everything I saw in Japan reminded me of something similar in China. Toshogu Shrine in Nikko, Nijo Castle in Kyoto, and Osaka

Castle in Osaka undoubtedly display the architectural style of the Tang Dynasty. The karamon embellished with a heavily carved and dazzlingly decorated bargeboard can be translated as meaning “Chinese gate”. Room dividers inside the palace are illustrated with paintings that are comparable to those images of Tang people exhibited in the Beijing Palace Museum. Exploring the hauntingly beautiful forest where ancient giants stretched toward the sky was like traveling back in time. Someone out there was playing a Chinese zither. I walked toward it, turned a corner, started walking in a different direction, and then turned another corner, seeing more trees in the way before I realized that I did not know where the music was coming from. And when I entered Nishijin Textile Center, which is known for producing shimmering fabric from silk for noble families in the old days, how could I get Jiangning Silk Manufacturing House described by Cao Xueqin out of my head? The moment I fed my eyes on the Kintai Bridge, one of the three famous bridges built in the Tokugawa Period, I was convinced that the great bridge featured in the panoramic painting, *Along the River during the Qingming Festival*, is not too steep to afford ordinary walking.

Hold your horses, I kept reminding myself. But once an idea had taken hold in the brain, it was almost impossible to eradicate it. Things had gotten out of control and became worse. Standing on the lookout point of Kiyomizu-dera that was built using all-wood joints and fasteners without screws or nails, I could not help but remember the magnificent Temple of Heaven. At the entrance, as soon as I spotted the pair of traditional iron footwear and the rusted metal staff that is too heavy for most people to lift alone, I thought of Lu Zhishen. The vast grassed area of Koraku-en just called Fan Zhongyan to mind. I recited softly, “Be the first one in my country to shoulder responsibility; be the last one to enjoy the fruits of labor.” Upon entering Sanjusangen-do, which contains one thousand statues of Kannon and eighteen grotesque statues of guardian deities, I asked myself if the Yungang Grottoes are cut from the same cloth. While I went into the freezing Akiyoshi Stalactite Cave, where groundwater and stalactites of different forms and shapes sprang a surprise, I was reminded that the Seven Star Crags in Guilin are second to none.

***

Maybe, I had barked up the wrong tree. It is nobody's fault that Chinese culture had exerted an enormous impact on nearly all aspects of life in Japan. In Lok Ma Chau, a breeze is picking up. With the Mainland stretching out right in front of me, I feel a deep yearning for my country. "The sun is closer; Changan City is too far away." I have never crossed the border. Who is to blame?

September 17, 1971

A Whispering Brook at Nanzen-ji

The weather has been sultry as the dog days of summer approach. Chilled tofu with a sprinkling of white sesame seeds and finely chopped spring onions is calling me. I have bought a block of tofu, and begin to cut it into slices. It boasts the highest water content. The texture is so smooth that it seems to have been strained through silk. I marvel at this soft, creamy wonder lying in my palm, and all at once I have a flashback to August 30, 1973, the day I had Yu-Tofu at Nanzen-ji in Japan.

***

Nanzen-ji represents the land of ultimate bliss. It is a Buddhist temple where believers are awakened to the Zen teachings such as: "First there is a mountain, then there is no mountain, and finally there is a mountain again. First there is a river, then there is no river, and finally there is a river again." An aqueduct that blends into the scenery of the spacious grounds forms part of a canal, following the Philosopher's Path to the neighboring prefecture. Whenever Professor Tang Junyi traveled to Kyoto, he patronized a restaurant that sat inside a beautiful sub-temple. He never missed out on the signature Nanzen-ji Yu-Tofu. Made at a traditional tofu shop, the Kyoto variety is regarded as the best in Japan, since the city has the purest drinking water and grows the highest quality soybeans. Not only did Professor Tang enjoy the lovely custard-like texture and seductive fresh flavor of the dish, but he also took pleasure in casting his eyes over the exquisite garden with Zen ambiance, where trees perform as a ground cover in full shade. He liked to quote from Shi Zhenlin: "Lack of intensity is delightful".

That day, Professor and Mrs. Tang brought me to the restaurant. On a knee-high table, there was a large-sized ceramic pot placed over low heat. Quietly, tofu was simmering in the pot. The most common mistake people make is allowing water to reach a rolling boil. In a small porcelain bowl, the white tofu was served with light soy sauce, which appeared to complement rather than compete with each other. I took a taste. It had a beany flavor, but immediately I found it spell boring. I was wondering if the restaurant owner had bought the food really cheaply and then overcharged us for it.

In Kyoto, the incessant screeching of cicadas during the day and cackling of frogs in the night caused a nuisance in the summertime. While I began to feel stressed out by the noise level, Professor Tang sat cross-legged and remained silent. "Can you hear a brook?" he asked, completely without warning. I cocked my head, listening. True to form, amidst the cicada's sound, I heard faintly the water dribble at a distance.

He gazed up at a work of calligraphy hung at the entrance gate of the temple, which I did not notice until now. It read: "WHISPER OF DHARMA BY A BROOK".

"The sounds of brooks flowing are the sounds of nature, period. So, where does dharma come from? It must come from the heart. 'Lack of intensity is delightful, but lack of mildness is upsetting.' " he said. The same quote appears in *Experiences of Life*. When he wrote this book, he had reached a higher spiritual level. His heart was calm and undisturbed.

A jaded person cannot see the things that are, because he is always looking for things that are not. To me, Yu-Tofu tasted bland, because I was used to sweet, salty, sour, and bitter tastes, and lost my sense of the mild taste. Moreover, the irritating noise made by cicadas had covered the soothing sound of a brook, because I failed to quiet internal noise and did not focus on the existing nature sounds around me. Only then did I know that I had a fixed mindset. I had been making troubles for myself all along.

Somebody with a fixed mindset loses the sense of sight, the sense of hearing, the sense of taste, and the sense of smell. Without the senses, the eye does not see, the ear does not hear, the tongue does not perceive any taste, and inevitably the view he adopts for himself narrows. He does not seek out experiences that will stretch him. Instead, he confines himself within the limits marked out by his own self. Professor Tang wanted me to listen to a brook and discover a whole new world.

***

I finish slicing tofu. I scoop some into my mouth and eat it without dipping sauce. A soy flavor is present, but I need to concentrate the mind in order to properly savor it. I give the mouthful of tofu time to pass over each taste bud. I work my way through the entire palate. Then, it slides down my throat like silky satin. It goes down smooth and easy all the way until it reaches the stomach.

This is how dharma whispers, like what it did amidst the screeching of cicadas at Nanzen-ji almost four decades ago. Professor Tang's favorite quote echoes in my ears. Today, in a cauldron of conflicting opinions boiling up all over this city, there is no time to waste regaining the sense of hearing.

August, 2010

Rambling Thoughts on Kyoto

I promise myself not to let Kyoto cross my mind. Then comes autumn and I know what that means…

***

That autumn in Kyoto, Arashiyama hid behind a veil of mist. I could not help but wonder: Did a fine drizzle fall on the lone traveler[5] when he showed up several decades ago? Did he climb up the broken stone stairs and crane his neck to have a look at the Katsura River? Did he ascend the steep slope and find his way to Daihikaku Senko-ji?

Located halfway up a mountain, the main hall of Senko-ji bore the impress of sadness deeper than usually perceived. The torii had seen better days. The temple bell was neglected. In this temple lived an old monk. "Oh, China! I had been there," he said to me quietly. And then he chuckled. Somehow he managed to shatter the sorrow of the ancient temple. He called to mind Ganjin in Nara.

Ganjin attempted to travel from China to Japan five times before the Rebellion of the Tang Dynasty. During that period of time, An Lushan first served as an officer of the Pinglu Army and later the governor of Hedong Circuit. Unfortunately, Ganjin had been forced to abandon all his expeditions due to unfavorable sea conditions. "I'm determined to cross the sea and propagate the Buddhist faith in Japan. And I'll die trying if necessary," he said, holding the hand of his first disciple, Puzhao, while tears ran down his cheeks. On his sixth attempt, he finally succeeded. But he went blind as a result of his hardship. At the end of the day, did he instill into the people any rules for enlightenment?

---

[5] Translator's note: It was Zhou Enlai, the first Premier of the People's Republic of China.

***

As a humble Earthling, quite honestly, I fail to understand why it was so important for Ganjin to spare no effort in passing on the teachings of Buddhism in an island country on the other side of the ocean.

Aw, it is difficult to think of a body of open water without bringing the Moon Crossing Bridge back into my mind…

***

As the evening wore on, the moon rose higher. A thousand-year-old pine tree stood on the southern side of the Moon Crossing Bridge to give me a warm welcome. Its reflection was undulating in the river. When I took a walk toward the ancient tree across the bridge, I felt like making my way toward the rising moon. The bridge, as its name suggests, lived up to its promise. How long did it take for the bridge builder to survey the Katsura basin before he decided on its current location? Had he been inspired by the poetic works of Kibi no Asomi Makibi, a scholar who had studied in Tang China?

Before I crossed the bridge, I strolled along the shore. I took a break under a tree. A stone tablet was erected, overlooking the river. On its face, a stark warning was carved: "NO MORE WAR BETWEEN JAPAN AND CHINA". If one had asked how long it had been there, it would have been a question with an obvious answer. Instead, one should have asked: How much blood had been shed? How many history books would have been needed to record the horrors of war?

***

Again, as a humble Earthling, I fail to understand the complicated story of the past. And please, I want to hear none of it, lest my heart break; my heart hate. No nation aspires to go to war, and yet there was a war. How many people had been killed? Do not ask me. Ask the stone tablet.

Before my mind's eye, the stone tablet on the shore is chilled. It makes no reply. Alas, Kyoto has crossed my mind again…

November 11, 1978

The Kyoto Tanka

"Shall we visit Kyoto together?" You ask softly in Japanese. You have learned that phrase in the language class.
This short essay is for you. This is meant to give my stay in Kyoto a fulfilling sense of closure.

***

Plum Blossoms at Kitano Tenmangu Shrine

People do not go to psychics to predict the peak blooming dates, for the Plum Blossom Festival is always held on February 25 every year.

The city was free of snow. I hopped on a bus, and asked for directions twice before I found my way to the Shrine. I was mildly surprised to find the place deserted. A few flowering trees looked desolate. In the absence of a flowing stream, it was difficult to transport their dreams to the ends of the world.

Sakura Flowers at Kiyomizu-dera

I clambered up the stairs to reach the lookout point of the Temple. The waters from a waterfall are divided into three streams. Legend has it that they possess the power to grant wishes for fortune, for career success, and for longevity respectively. However, I forwent the pleasure of drinking water from any of the streams. As a passing traveler, I did not have a deep-down burning desire to get rich, to succeed, nor to live longer.

The green mountain blushed after it drank in the charm of spring. No wonder it always stayed young.

I loitered on inside the Temple.

The Temple cuddled up to the mountain.

The mountain stood amidst the misty clouds of pinkish hue.

However, the breeze was unscented. Sakura flowers had kept their distance. Their delicate petals had fallen off somewhere else.

Bonfire Noh Performance at Heian Shrine

Against the backdrop of the setting sun, the Shrine, which features sweeping slopes with upturned eaves, had lost its warmth. The tiled corners felt chilly on an early summer evening. Somehow the hanging metallic baskets of flaming firewood were almost forbidding.

There were no theater drapes on stage, hence a performance without a beginning and an ending. The whimpering, monotonous quality of the chant seemed smashed to smithereens, its broken pieces lying all over the place. Actors, wearing wooden masks and dressed in long, loose costumes, performed short sequences of dance-like movements with an air of solemnity. Who were behind the masks? Was the Prince of Lanling[6] one of them?

The Gion Festival

A huge crowd gathered in the street, waving their round paper fans as if to invite summer into the city. The pattering sound of their steps made by the clogs was no more than an overture to the Gion Matsuri. Musicians were sitting in magnificent yama and hoko parade floats. The melody they played was simple. Their instruments, mainly the flute, the gong chime, and the small cymbal, followed a stereotypical pattern without much variation. But their music said many a prayer in thanksgiving.

The lights were too bright. At a little distance, two old men sat on a bench. They were uninterested in this raucous street party. Faintly aloof, they took in all the sights but did not speak a word.

A Street Lined with Maidenhair Trees

At times, the living world was uncaring.

Unloved, the street was littered with yellowish or brownish leaves. A maidenhair tree in bare and skeletal branch had a similar appearance to an immense handheld fan. A leaf sighed when it was carried away by a current of autumn air. I figured that it had a bitter-sweet love story to tell.

---

[6] Translator's note: The opera *Prince Lanling in Battle* was introduced from China to Japan during the Tang Dynasty.

Someone was burning leaves. A despondent curl of smoke rose. The leaves were reluctant to bid farewells to their loved ones even when they were on their way out. Year after year, the westerly winds send the locals a poignant reminder of the passing of time.

Kozan-ji Lit up by Maple Leaves

Fine wine helped in bringing a drunken glow to the maples in the mountain. They all turned brilliant red.

The maples were completely void of poetic words as far as I could see. I picked up a couple of them and stashed them away in my kimono sleeve.

Tradition dictates that visitors toss a white clay disk down the cliff. As they do it, they make a wish to return to the Temple. I left without making a promise.

The Fire Festival at Kurama-dera

I turned up my coat collar to meet the wind. However, I was not into climbing the ninety-nine steps leading up to the Temple.

This evening, people chose to parade rather than pray to the guardian angel of Rakuhoku. Holding up huge pine torches, they ran up the stairs in a frenzy of excitement. Loud chants were heard. The fires were kept burning. A shadow of primitive human desires was flickering over the sea of faces.

I did not feel I could truly belong. Sparks were flying out of the torches in the night sky that was darker than black ink.

Fresh Snow Falling in Mount Hiei

Mount Hiei might be standoffish, but it had the heart of a lovesick maiden, whose hair turns stark white overnight because of sorrows. Wait no more and go see snow on the Mountain, people urged. And so I went. I called on the frosty soul.

Snow was fleet of foot. The whole mountain was lost in thought. I found myself cast adrift on my first pilgrimage to the holy place.

At the Enriro Temple Hall, I did not burn incense on the altar. Instead, I bought a sacred book in pursuit of enlightenment – all is vanity.

On New Year's Eve, 1981

Sakura Flowers and the Samurai Sword

April sashays along. The weather has been alternating between dull drizzle and dazzling sunshine. I miss the sakura waning on cherry trees in Japan…

***

One day, I took a break from reading to go for a walk, feasting my eyes on masses and masses of pinkish flowers of weeping cherry. Long and slender, the waving branches bore cascades of double blossoms which were nearly pure white but tinged with the palest pink. They touched almost to the lawn, like those of weeping willow, except that they were more timid and shier. The spring picnic under a canopy of blooms was also a joy to behold. When a light breeze came up, thousands and thousands of dancing petals descended on my overcoat. I was nonplussed by the unexpected distraction.

***

It is its fleeting beauty that makes weeping cherry special. Without much regret, the flowers fall from the tree in total silence, catching the sightseer completely off-guard. While the waxing and waning of flowers is an ever-present part of nature, it saddens the heart if they are associated with friendship.

***

On the bank of the Oi River, I perched on a rock. Someone told me a story about the samurai sword.

During the Kamakura Period, Masamune was the greatest swordsmith. However, where the sharpness of the blade was concerned, it seemed that his apprentice, Muramasa, continued to surpass him.

In an attempt to see which blade was significantly sharper, two swords, one forged by Muramasa, another by Masamune, were held upright in a rivulet. Both blades were facing the water that flowed toward them. And what happened? While all of the fallen leaves carried by the current downstream toward the Muramasa sword were neatly cut in half, those drifting along toward the Masamune sword made sudden swerves, changed their direction, and moved away. Muramasa did not win. His sword with its razor-sharp cutting edge was only designed for thrusting and slashing. By contrast, Masamune had the last laugh. While his sword was a weapon intended for killing, it spared the lives of the innocent. It had human qualities. It was more than just a sword.

I spent a little while lounging on the riverbank. In my head, I could imagine that the Masamune sword was placed in the river. Quietly, leaves drifted by. I did not see any menacing light reflecting off the edge of the blade.

***

The sword is a weapon. Its blade has to be skillfully forged so that it will hold a keen edge. Masamune committed his soul into his sword but at the same time, he took a laissez-faire attitude to life. It is admirable that one kills only when absolutely necessary.

His sword should be set on a pedestal.

April 30, 1979

Japanese Hand-Towels

A friend of mine has brought back a piece of wrapping cloth for me after a visit to Toshodai-ji in Nara. Dyed with old-fashioned, fine-detailed patterns, it calls the Japanese hand-towel to mind.

Furoshiki are a type of wrapping cloth traditionally used to hand-carry goods. They were a common sight on the street in the country before the advent of plastic bags, and even before environmental protection became a concern. In recent years, they have been replaced with canvas tote bags. Maybe, young users, both male and female, have trouble tying tight furoshiki knots. They simply stop trying and give up. Nevertheless, hand-towels are still popular in Japan.

Hand-towels are usually made of pure cotton, but the design of the print may vary. Each towel measures about thirty-four by eighty (or ninety) centimeters in size. When folded evenly in half, it looks like a scarf. While it often doubles as a sweatband, a neckerchief, or a head-covering in summer, it is an item used for multiple purposes, such as to clean a wet area, to wipe away one's sweat, to shield one's scalp from the scorching sun, to bundle things up, and to keep one warm in winter.

As a research fellow, I spent some time at the Kyoto University Research Center for the Cultural Sciences more than thirty years ago. The old library building was not air-conditioned. Only a few fans were wheezing when the temperature climbed up to twenty-eight degree Celsius in summer. The insufferable heat during the afternoon made the room stiflingly hot, and most people were nodding off. I learned from Mori (a librarian) a trick that made life easier. I bought myself a white hand-towel. I thoroughly wetted it through under a cold tap in the toilet, and tied it around my neck. Immediately I felt a refreshing coolness seep over me. And when the towel got warm in about fifteen minutes, I scurried off to commence the whole procedure again. Just like that, I had embraced the heat in the cool company of my hand-towel. To this day, I still do the same trick to lower my core temperature when I take a vacation during the summer months. For sure my traveling companions have seen me drape a wet towel around the neck, or wipe my face with it.

Hand-towels are not a part of the locals' attire in Hong Kong, but I often bring back several of them whenever I visit Japan – no, not so much using them as reminding myself of a time long past. Today, they come in a variety of patterns, beautifully dyed in a wide range of colors. Yet, they are not as smooth as the inexpensive, plain-woven, pure-cotton one I still keep from my Kyoto days. Much as it has turned yellowish, it was once lovingly softened by my tender feelings for that particular city many summers ago.

June 14, 2009

That Evening

We went out for a stroll in the evening. With its crisp air, mid-summer felt so different in Kyoto.

Like a phantom from the past, Nijo Castle illuminated with floodlights continued to haunt people in modern times. And the hotel where we stayed overnight was right across the street!

As expected, the street was quiet at such a late hour. I knew that the last bus was yet to come, for an old woman sitting on a wooden bench next to the bus stop was fanning herself languidly. Her eyes fixed ahead toward the distance. Not surprisingly, leisure was a state of mind. This neighborhood was not a tourist attraction, as it was nothing out of the ordinary. All shops were shut for the night, except a supermarket that stayed open twenty-four hours. Since it was a new-age business idea, we were curious, and decided to take a look. The moment we entered the shop, a familiar aroma that did not belong in the place wafted out. My, oh, my, it was *inakani* (farm food)! Turnips, fish balls, and the like were cooked in a pot of simmering broth. They were all comfort foods in winter to help one beat the cold weather. Why on earth were they on sale now in an air-conditioned supermarket at this time of year? Much as we just had a big meal, it was difficult to outsmart temptation. We used hand gestures to communicate with the shopkeeper, who was considerate enough to put two pairs of chopsticks and a few tiny bags of grated wasabi in our takeaway box. I held it close to my chest as we continued our walk.

The street was lined with shops in low, wooden buildings. All were dark inside but one. A yellow lamp hung over the closed door. I gasped. There, in the display windows, faint lights illuminated a wide variety of *origami* Sleeping Cats! It was almost eleven in the evening, and of course business was not as usual. Holy cow! What am I going to do? Desire seemed to have the upper hand. I would not let the opportunity pass me by! I paced up and down in exasperation. I believed that the owner lived behind his store (which is common practice in Kyoto), and had a gut feeling that he was hospitable and helpful (like all owners of local shops). Moreover, there was a notice on the door that read: "PLEASE RING BELL FOR ASSISTANCE". Wai knew me inside out, I never took no for an answer. So, she buzzed the bell.

The silhouette of a man moved behind a partition. Then, a man of middle age appeared. The crucial moment came when I pointed to the assortment of different Sleeping Cat models on display. He nodded, and smiled gently to put me at ease. He walked toward the door as he buttoned his coat.

That was how I became the proud owner of three *origami* cats!

If we had not visited Kyoto, or if I had not had faith in the locals, or if Wai had not taken the bull by the horns, this story would have had a different ending. LOL!!!

September 9, 1997

The Mid-Summer Song

1

A big blue sky always made my day.

The sunlight glittered. Fresh grass and young saplings had fun without lingering worry.

Two butterflies were fluttering their wings. They just met. Every now and then they rested on a low fence. For sure, they had never heard The Butterfly Lovers before.

White clouds, like a Beijing opera dancer's sleeves, billowed against the blue sky. Somehow the beast of summer heat was tamed.

I sat on a long veranda in the afternoon, knitting a carefree dream, and lounging the day away.

Alas, those days have been lost for no reason at all. Since when did it happen?

2

A friend, who has the gift of poetic thought, traveled a hundred miles to rendezvous with the late afternoon sky.

He was angling for sunset clouds scattered from above and all around like peach blossoms. He intended to unfold a paper scroll brilliantly illuminated, and read the best song verses of all time penned by prevailing westerly winds. When golden daylight changed water from a murmuring brook into wine, he would dip a ladle in it and drink. He would watch tow-colored pigeons flying random loops, while listening to an oriole's love story. She had just returned home from the far side of the world.

Sadly, he only found dark and heavy clouds pile up on the horizon like massive mountains. The large stretches of country woke up from a bad dream, looking dazed and confused.

He was at a loss. And then he remembered a line by a Song poet: "A few cheerless evenings, subdued and sad/Carried within themselves, a lifetime's distress".

3

The thought of barge haulers is always disturbing. Aren't oars and sails used to steer a boat through the water? Why is there a gang of men dragging a barge on the banks of a river?

Barge haulers walk barefoot on the banks. Pebbles, which were once jagged rocks, are now worn smooth by the trudging of their tired feet. The grass is soaked through their sweat. It withers.

YO, HEAVE HO! YO, HEAVE HO! They holler, as days and weeks and months and years drift away on the water. They follow the river on the path of life, in the knowledge that the barge is heavily loaded with their fruits of labor. But they are only strangers. Will people remember a single feature of their face?

August 31, 1982

The Autumn Song

Lethargy

Autumn is a season of indolence.

I seldom pass time without taking part in purposeful activity, even when spring exhales gloomy mists with monotonous regularity, when summer heat covers the land like a lid on a casserole dish, and when the winter chill pricks my skin with hundreds of needles. Only at this time of year am I propelled into idleness. I open the door and step into cool, crisp morning air. The sky is a wide expanse of unbroken blue painted with wax crayon. Autumn has crept up on me, and I did not hear its footsteps. Now it casts a spell over me.

A few years ago, a friend and I idled away a couple of autumnal months together. These days we live our lives in the fast lane, and most of the time we hardly touch base with each other. Having said that, she customarily sends me a note every year when autumn is in full swing. It is almost as if to keep a promise she has made to me. Something just jolts her memory. She writes about her yearning for the time we spent together in playful words. There is no need to write back, because great minds think alike.

Those who have a job can hardly afford the luxury of indulging in nostalgia. Nostalgia is a disease, so to speak. For years, I have been trying to discover a cure, but nothing pans out. Oh well, I may just act on a poet's advice – "Flaming maples drink and get drunk/Fresh daisy flowers stay in deep, deep sleep." I will let nature take its course.

Trees

How can I ever forget the impressive avenue lined with full-grown maidenhair trees, where the perfume of osmanthus flowers settled subtly on my clothing!

I lifted my head and gazed up into the canopy of maidenhair trees. The leaves are shaped like a heart, or a butterfly, for that matter. They were yellowing. I was completely captivated by their soft color, which was almost transparent to all visible light. It seemed to me that the trees would keep their leaves for a little while, but I did not know that fall foliage was coming. With a sigh, I soon realized they fell off trees within a matter of days, drifting in the air like a prodigal son walking out the door.

Over here, there was the scratching sound of a leaf rake.

Over there, someone was burning leaves, or burning dreams in the eye of a poet. A few wisps of smoke were rising toward the uppermost branches, as if in death, fallen leaves and trees became whole again in body and soul. Life would go on. Spring would return next year. And it was a promise.

Death is just part of the natural cycle of life. Life never ends.

On my life's journey, I have seen a long line of trees this autumn. Some have leaves wilting or turning yellow, the others look like they are dying. Sadly, all of them are saplings, and none of them are advanced in years. That being the case, nature's love will always live. All goes onward and outward, nothing collapses, as a poet observes.

October 17, 1976

Postlude: The Autumn Song

A friend of mine parceled up a bunch of white reeds and sent it over by air mail. It came as a pleasant surprise. The delivery was aggressive. Some of the white, fluffy seed heads have broken off their stems. It's not something you could put in the mail, you silly goose! I mutter as I stare down at the plants. A memory is jogged loose…

It was a fine autumn day. My friend and I had gone up into the hill country to explore fall foliage of maple trees. On our trip back, we decided to take advantage of the charming weather and goof around instead of putting our feet up.

Once we had made up our mind, we folded away the map and roamed from field to field. As we rounded a corner, a massive bed of reeds all of a sudden – I repeat, all of a sudden – opened up before our eyes. It was absolutely phenomenal! We had never seen reed stalks that long and seed heads that white! The whole place was like an open-top sheer chiffon curtain hung from the sky. The dense thicket of reeds billowed out around us in the breeze, and took our breath away. While the maple leaves had managed to get under our skin, this was something else.

The air was perfumed far and near by the sweet scent of grass. It was a perfect place to play hide-and-seek. It would be fun, no? Nah – we were too old for that kind of game. So, we sat in silence amidst the reeds, while downy tufts of seeds scattered our heads and coats.

"Remember Lu Li's poem? 'Autumn is a half-sigh/Of westerly winds, by oversight/Reeds seem troubled/Their hair turns white overnight.'

"One time, a friend sent Lu a single reed stalk in a vase. 'Guess what I bought you! It's autumn!' he said. Lu kept it in his study, but held fast to it in his dreams."

We started sharing stories about reeds we had heard or read. My friend broke off a hollow stalk, using it to make a simple wind instrument. She blew it. It did not produce any sound. But she seemed intent on taking it home. I teased her about it. As a mere mortal, she was not supposed to play a flute meant for the fairy. She laid the blame on me. Her beautiful flute was totally shocked soundless and speechless by my horribly boring stories…

We both miss that place tremendously but we have not returned to it. While geographical distance becomes an excuse, the underlying reason is that we are torn between several lovers: white reeds, blonde maidenhair trees, brilliant maple leaves, and golden mums.

There is distance in space and there is distance in time. The reeds in my hand look tenderer than those we saw together in the wild. On this chilly, gloomy winter day, autumn is delivered belatedly.

Reeds, like common plants, only prosper in nature. Once confined within a vase, they are locked inside a dream they never wake up from. They weep. They become ever more sorrowful. I put them back in the box, uncertain what to do.

I meant to write one more essay about autumn – consider the job done!

January 17, 1977

The Winter Song

Adagio

Winter is a melody to be played at a slow tempo.

The sky is comparable to a ceiling that has paint peeling from it. Only when the sun shines through the clouds do I realize that there is nothing more depressing than to get through a gray day.

On a pier, there are seven green wooden benches bathed in the sunlight. As the afternoon rolls around, the whole place becomes "alive". By "alive", I do not mean it is like the kind of "liveliness" you find near the five flag-poles on Tsim Sha Tsui Ferry Pier in Hong Kong. This neighborhood – if I must come up with an analogy – is like a sequence of slow-motion movie scenes. The elderly sitting on the wooden benches are quiet, low-key people who embrace their silver-fox status in a modest way. They probably have a glamorous past, but they do not talk about it like a blowhard. Two of them begin nodding from drowsiness slowly and almost rhythmically. The others sit bolt upright, deeply engaged in conversation. Those who are being talked to are attentive; those who do the talking are prim and proper. Their wrinkled faces hardly give away any hint of what they are talking about. Is it something worth celebrating or something worth crying over? Maybe, it is worth neither celebrating nor crying over. Or, maybe, their feelings have become lusterless with time. They have moved beyond rain and storm and calm and sunshine, and now they are at peace with themselves. To them, the past is nothing but a coat of paint that peels off.

As the wintry light fades, they remain deep in conversation. An evening song is being performed adagio.

The Big Dipper

The asterism is located in the far reaches of the universe. Its name went back to Arabian usage from ancient times, where people believed that the four stars of the constellation defined a "coffin" while the other three defined the "mourners". Under the chilly sky in a vast barren desert, there seemed to be plenty of opportunity to look on the black side.

In ancient China, however, people were more hopeful. They were convinced that the seven stars represented seven heavenly gods, each of whom was assigned responsibility for the day-to-day management of the world's business. "The gods reside at the center of the sky. They have in place the four cardinal directions. They have control over the four seasons and five elements." In other words, the gods were in charge of yin-yang, environmental impacts, natural forces, national government, agriculture, and military affairs. While lesser mortals were not given the reins of their own destiny, they were entitled to act naïve. To pin their hopes on an asterism a hundred light-years away definitely made life easier.

In modern times, the Big Dipper helps a disoriented sailor or traveler find the North Star in the night sky. However, on a dark, stormy night when the asterism hides behind heavy clouds, one's life choices are hanging in the balance.

I gaze at the serene sky. The Big Dipper does not belong in a winter's night. Ultimately, natural laws of science are not to be challenged. Sigh.

February 14, 1977

The Spring Song

Yellow Dust

The newspaper reports that dust from the desert regions of China is whisked by strong winds into the atmosphere and travels to Japan. It is kousa! All at once, something I have almost forgotten pops into my head…

It was a spring morning in Kyoto. Before I went to school, habitually I gazed out at Mount Hiei. It was capped by lower cloud and shrouded in a thick mist. I made a mental note to take my well-worn, black umbrella with me. There was sunlight on the street, but the sun was tired, as though it was getting a cold. A yellowish haze had blanketed the city. It was some freak of nature suggestive of both mist and dust. Because of this fogginess, the sun actually looked like the moon, and you could stare directly at it. Ominous clouds were gathering overhead, which looked more menacing than a hailstorm. My glasses were covered with a film of soil particles. My eyes itched. I removed my glasses, and wiped the lenses carefully. I felt apprehensive for the rest of the day. As a stranger in this city, I thought that a natural catastrophe was imminent.

When I returned to the dormitory in the late afternoon, I saw all residents going about their daily business as usual. "What kind of weather is it?" I asked, yielding to curiosity. "It's the kousa season. The sky's clotted with ten thousand miles of yellow dust," the warden replied. In order to avoid misunderstandings, she wrote "ten thousand miles of yellow dust" in kanji characters on a piece of paper…

The warden's handwriting immediately leaps to my eye although four years have passed since that day.

Foliage

Flowers are fine, but I take a greater liking for green foliage of a plant.

It is springtime. Barren trees are showing signs of promise. The scene is on fast-forward. There is nothing wishy-washy about it. Spring. Is.

Here. I only have myself to blame for overwhelming my life with work. Looking at budding trees every morning when I leave for work, I say to myself that time flies on fleeting wings and that is the mystery of life. A lot of things have passed in a fast-motion sequence before we realize it. We look, but do not see. It is a flaw in human nature.

When fresh grass sprouts and young leafage grows, life explodes. At the sight of it, we become excited. Our eyes are opened. Life is not something of an enigma, nor is it a depressing dream. It is just that time is an impatient director who rushes us off to a new scene every day. But who cares as long as we deliver a performance and give it our best shot?

A leaf reaches maturity only because it strove for growth yesterday.

April 4, 1977

And So Entered Spring...

We are blessed to live in Hong Kong.

Absorbed in our mundane tasks, we are totally oblivious of the turning of the wheel of time. Be that as it may, people who have a vulnerability to depression tend to feel sad on New Year's Eve. Some are hit by a pang of worry when they spot their very first silver strand of hair. Others are in distress when they wise up to the fact that while their kids are growing up, they are growing old themselves. But most of us get so busy with our daily lives that we do not take the time necessary to be introspective. We are unaware of the passage of time, as if we were locked up in a room without windows day and night, being cut off from the outside world for years.

I am a Hongkonger born and bred. Perhaps, as a newbie, I made a blunder by visiting Kyoto where the four seasons are easily distinguishable. Life force energy surges through the tips of trees and the blades of grass in early spring. No doubt about it! A gust of wind or a drop of rain may instantly challenge my perception in various landscape settings before I know it. Since I grew up in the land of "no seasons", my personal experience in this city has been a pleasant encounter touched by a tinge of sadness.

It is not worth going into the details of how excited I was when I woke up to morning light and saw snow through the windows for the first time in my life. Instead, I will start with what I have seen in Kyoto since the spring equinox.

Two days of light rain brought a spell of warm weather. Finally the rain let up. It was surprising to see that the weeping willows on both sides of the street were lavished with young leaves. Tree budding is as fragile as silence – when you say its name, you break it. The cherry blossom season had been eagerly anticipated throughout the winter months. Then, just after the arriving warm air had stayed for the whole day, the sakura trees burst into flower almost overnight. The canopy was spectacular. It was dazzling! As a stranger in the city, I made an uneducated guess on my way to school that the flowers would only stay for around two weeks. Easy come, easy go! Right?

The long street was bathed in pale pink light. *Chop-chop! Go see the cherry blossoms before it's too late!* The locals urged. They suggested places like Heian Shrine, Maruyama Park, Kiyomizu-dera, and the Kyoto Botanical Garden. One single cherry flower in solitude was certainly nondescript. However, seen from a distance, masses and masses of overhanging cherry flowers became banks and banks of rosé, dreamy clouds floating around the hillside. I went for a stroll on a path. I felt the brush of the plantings against my hair as I parted the overhead branches of weeping willows and cherry trees. However, I seemed too distracted to give them their share of attention, as I was utterly amazed at how the locals took part in rowdy picnics. From morning till evening, they ate and drank. The entire place was all lit up with paper lanterns after dark.

And then, on the fourth evening, light showers and blustering winds came without warning. They continued through the night. The next morning, fleshy blossoms floated off the trees like snow with the ebb and flow of the winds, scattering over the shoulders of people who happened to pass by before dropping to the ground. It was only then that I was thunderstruck by their beauty entangled in the softness of sadness. I took a rather circuitous route to school, in order to avoid walking on the carpet of fallen flowers. Oharame[7], who wore traditional farm clothing and carried a bamboo broom, were seen throughout the city trying to pick up the broken pieces.

Sure enough, the blooming period was a brief window. Green leafage – shiny and definitely seductive – has emerged to present a fresh look of the city. It wows the locals. Other kinds of flowers, like, azaleas, wisteria's flowers, and tulips, will come and go in a jiffy, thus making life difficult for those who wish to catch up with them. Now, people begin to get the rain gear ready. When the rainy season comes, they cannot wait to visit Saiho-ji, which is famed for its moss garden. Chop-chop!

I used to wonder if the melancholy tone that characterizes much classical poetry in literature is genuine, but now my doubts are cleared

---

[7] The village of Ohara is located in the northern outskirts of Kyoto. The women, clad in a traditional blue and white costume, are called *Oharame*. They make a living in the city by doing manual labor, such as cleaning streets and mowing a lawn.

up. Indeed, the rapid changes in nature have deeply touched many a heart over the centuries. The cherry blossom viewing season is used by an unseen hand as a vehicle to impart profound knowledge to those who recognize that the world spins too fast. And rightly so, moving away from Hong Kong makes me feel that life is speeding up.

Kyoto, July, 1973

Part III

Again and again,
My glass is raised,
By the window facing east,
A cup of solitude I drain.
— Tao Yuanming

A Letter from Hong Kong

June 29, 2002

Dear Pauline and Kit,

I meant to write you back in early July, 1997 when Hong Kong was bracing herself for change. It would have been a decently long letter, for you guys always remain loyal no matter the distance or time that separates you from her, plus I had so much to report. Sadly, lightning struck out of a blue sky, and my thoughts got all jumbled up. As days went by, the city was plunged into agitation, unrest, and confusion, which put me in a difficult position. I was a diehard. I could never start writing anything unless a reasonable point in question was proved, enough information was gathered, and everything was in order. It was only natural that I did not write that letter.

On June 30, 1997, I did a damn silly thing. In Central, I took a bus to Kennedy Town and back again. I hopped on another bus to go to Happy Valley, and from there, I got on yet another bus that took me to Shau Kei Wan. In other words, I had cruised along the main road from West to East that runs parallel to the northern coast of the Island. Like I said, it was a damn silly thing. Lilian Lee, a local novelist and sentimentalist, was smarter. She chose to go for a tram ride — you remember, it was the locals' most popular pastime when we were in our teens. I love the tram. I love the sound it makes when it honks the tinkling bell. Yet, I took a bus instead of a tram on that special occasion. Don't you think it was strange? Later, after I read Lee's *Tram Tour on June 30*, I just kicked myself for making such a mistake. In retrospect, I subconsciously resisted the idea of a tram ride that day, the reason being that most of the trams had replaced the tinkling bell with a tooting horn. To people from the older generations, the clear ting-ting is associated with unhurriedness, prudence, and also a touch of melancholy, especially when a tram returns to the depot at midnight. Listening to it is a trip down memory lane amidst the hustle and bustle of a city. The tooting horn simply does not fit the conventional image of a tram.

On July 25, 1997, I went to the Immigration Department located in Harbor Building to pick up my passport issued by the government of the Hong Kong Special Administrative Region of the People's Republic of China. In a poignant moment, I got so emotional that I could hardly hold back my tears in front of a junior civil servant. All the way home I sniveled. As soon as I got home, I had a photo of myself taken, wearing a stupid grin on my face while holding up the passport that uses a deep blue cover with words printed in a golden color. Just for the record! Considering that I used to hold a British National (Overseas) passport, and had to reluctantly declare that I was a British Dependent Territories citizen on the immigration entry form each time traveling abroad, the few drops of tears shed in the Immigration Department and the smile captured in the photo spoke a million words.

I have accepted a friend's invitation to view the fireworks extravaganza[8] from the Hong Kong Convention and Exhibition Center in Wan Chai tomorrow evening. I seldom attended the New Year's Eve fireworks show before 1997 because of claustrophobia in crowds. Once I was in the Mid-Levels neighborhood when the show was on. Half of the sky was lit up. When I heard the booming sounds, I had flashbacks to my experiences in times of war when Wan Chai was heavily bombed. That night, I dreamed that I escaped to the sea. On a boat, I turned around, and saw that the whole Wan Chai district had already been engulfed in flames. From that day forward, I had carefully avoided watching the spectacle live until 1997. (That year, there were many occasions where firecrackers were used.) For the past five years, I had been in the front line of the show. I felt the heat on my face when flames and sparks were falling in the sky over my head. My heart was thumping. Each time when fireworks shot across the sky, I cowered back, patting my chest. My heart was beating too fast, and yet my mind went blank. However, familiarity breeds contempt. I begin to find it monotonous. A fireworks display is nothing but a scene that consists of

[8] Translator's note: It is one of the celebration events to mark the anniversary of the establishment of the Hong Kong Special Administrative Region.

the most glorious moments that die down within seconds until only taciturnity remains.

When we speak on the phone, you guys always ask, "How are things going in Hong Kong?" In Toronto, you have got all the latest Hong Kong news on TV. How are things going in Hong Kong? I guess by that you mean to ask how I feel about certain things in Hong Kong, rather than what is happening in Hong Kong. "It's so hot here." "It's so humid here." "The air is so polluted. I need to cover my mouth and nose when I cross the street in Causeway Bay."… Since a long-distance phone call costs next to nothing, more and more people stop putting pen to paper. Gone are the days when a letter came in an envelope and was handwritten on a sheet of paper. These days you call abroad and shoot the breeze with a friend, it does not come back to bite you in the hip pocket.

I retired from teaching this year. Incidentally, the education system in Hong Kong is undergoing a sweeping reform. It has been under fire from all sides for years, and it certainly needs revamping for development and pedagogical purposes. But I feel funny about it.

Too many people deliver flowery speeches that do not hold water. Their grandiloquent expressions are baffling and bewildering. But no one, or should I say no specialist, hits the bull's-eye. There is no road map. Officials at all levels of the government make changes for the sake of making them. They are full of ideas. So-and-so or what's-his-name makes a few feints, and the rest get into a panic. "Interaction" between education officers, teachers, parents, and students drags on and on. Dedicated teachers are worn-out. When I see them hurry to a training session or forum, my heart aches for them. They are only pawns in the game but are forced into crossing the Rubicon under the new rules of the game.

Yes, I do feel funny about the whole thing. On the one hand, I concern myself with the reform. I hate to see it end up as neither fish nor fowl. On the other hand, it is none of my business, because I am no longer in a position to do anything. Should I just eat, drink, and be merry, shutting my ears to the bubbling cauldron of conflicting opinions? But then I have been married to my teaching job for several decades. Once the knot was tied, there is no way to untie it. So, it looks like — ahem — the joke is on me.

I have ended up rambling on in this letter. It may not be as formal as a report, but I guarantee the authenticity and credibility of the content.

Take care,

Siu Si

The Lost Tales of Hong Kong

Hong Kong is a city with an indistinct family background.

The indistinct family background is generally attributed to a past that has caused much distress. And the best remedy for distress is to obscure the true picture of it. Hongkongers are often criticized for lacking a sense of history. Such a remark does not have negative connotations in itself. If you pass by the Sung Wong Toi Garden, it is hard to imagine that the square-shaped stone memorial, which looks a bit inane now, is the remaining portion of a boulder originally large enough to provide ample space for several people standing atop it, let alone relate it to the historical story of the last boy emperor of the Song Dynasty, who climbed up onto it more than seven hundred years ago, looking out upon the sea while tears coursing down his cheeks.

Hong Kong is too busy to spend time looking back on the past. With all her might, she is moving forward, keeping pace with and adjusting herself to the high metabolic rate of global trends. This is her rhythm of life. Those who had spent a good part of their lives here and left not long ago sometimes lose their way in this once-familiar city upon their return. Like a stranger, they need to ask for directions when they are trying to find a place. Everything around them seems so foreign and unfamiliar. As things go, buildings were torn down before they reached a ripe old age. Elevated overpasses and some kind of Post-modern physical structures were erected.

I was born and raised in Hong Kong. Oftentimes I tell myself that it would be great if I can come up with some sweeping generalizations to define the characteristics of this city. My friends from overseas should probably find them interesting. However, it is easier said than done. Maybe, Hong Kong is ever-changing. Or maybe, I am always caught in a magic net interwoven with threads of strong emotion whenever I contemplate what this city is really like… Gee, there is love and there is hate. I think what happened to Wan Chai provides a clue to my love-hate relationship with Hong Kong.

It is not an exaggeration to say that Wan Chai is an old district that got into a fight over territory, since she had seized a large area of land reclaimed from the sea. Various changes have taken place over the years and left a strong aftertaste in the mouth of an old-timer. Buildings on Hennessy Road that were originally built on reclaimed land are now dilapidated. One by one they are on their way to be knocked down. Taller buildings that block the view to the sky were put up. Occasionally a decrepit low-rise is spotted, sandwiched between two brand-new high-rises, dying a slow death. It depicts such a sorry sight that there are times when I wish it dead. That said, I am thankful for its existence. It has been woven into my childhood memories. At one time, Lockhart Road and Jaffe Road had acquired a reputation as a red-light district because of the publication of a novel about Suzie Wong. Since then, the name of Wan Chai triggered all kinds of wild thoughts in the mind of a playboy from other countries. Each time a foreign navy ship dropped anchor in Victoria Harbor, I dreaded people talking about Wan Chai. I despised this old district where I grew up, but then I felt resentful when I heard people say bad things about her. And I would speak out in defense of her against all accusations. During my younger years, every commonplace street scene of this district was a heart-warming sight. But now she looks like a different person, leading a glamorous life amidst contemporary hotels and commercial buildings. I should be happy for her, but sadly there is not much left to hold us together. While her looks and her personality keep changing, my childhood memories begin to fade into insignificance.

The character of a city is defined by its cultural landscape. And what is the character of Hong Kong then? Some say that she is at a crossroads between the East and the West; others say that she is pretty much a cultural desert. Is she comparable to a handsome Junoesque woman? Or does she resemble a bitter woman with a gray face? How would you describe her? Unfortunately, no great master of realism has as yet managed to paint a meticulous picture of her. Meanwhile, those who call Hong Kong a cultural desert have been hooting their contempt for decades. Naturally, they do not take her seriously enough to conduct a formal investigation into her past. Do several millions of inhabitants really live in such an infertile desert? For decades, distinguished writers from up north or down south have passed through this city. Although they did not find their home here, they had ploughed up land during their stay and left their marks behind. (If that is the case, I wonder who is to blame for the desertification of the city.) Visitors and sojourners from culturally diverse backgrounds had planted a few trees here and a few shrubs there, and somehow they have turned this city into a mixed-species garden. It is the only one of its kind, where people from the Western world find the characteristics of the Orient are somewhat missing, while people from the Mainland believe that it is a city under the Occidental influence. And what do we Hongkongers say? Well, it is hard for us to describe our own city. On the one hand, we chin up and sail into the wind, taking the compliment that this is an international center for cultural exchange, but on the other hand we follow the crowd and agree meekly that this is a cultural desert. We do not care even if we are stung by the insulting remark, because we are survivors. And that is the way how Hong Kong has become a city that attracts the attention of the world.

Time flies without making a fuss. People of my generation wake up and smell the coffee. We now realize that our existence and our city's existence are connected and inseparable. Some of us had left for a colder country, but they cannot help casting a backward glance at this place where they once felt safe. The rest of us stay put. We start to take a better look at this piece of land where we had been nourished and nurtured. We begin to care about everything that is happening now. However, there is no time for us to trace our roots, for the journey ahead of us is too long.

When a friend is visiting Hong Kong, I often bring the guest to Victoria Peak in the evening, no, not so much promoting tourism (like the advertisement says, "There are splendid illuminations lavishly produced by hundreds of millions of dollars".) as seeing a kind of spectacular visual illusion. When we take the peak tram all the way to the top, we are impelled to sit with our backs straight against the back of the seat under the pull of gravity. All buildings on one side of the tramway appear to fall toward the summit as we turn our heads to get a view of the cityscape. In point of fact, we have a natural instinct for adjusting the body position to cope with a change of the subjective vertical caused by the tilted visual environment. But in doing so, we look at everything on lower land from a tilting angle. I usually fall silent by the time we reach the terminus. A blaze of light is lit up beneath us. Show, don't tell. Is there a better way to describe the luminosity in the evening sky from the lights of the city? I am all pleasantly feasting my eyes on the spectacular view while the out-of-towner exclaims in wonder.

The evening view of Hong Kong is bewitching. Layer upon layer of sparkling lights create all kinds of tints and tones and shades and, therefore, give a strong feeling of infinite depth. It always pleases me to partly close my eyes and squint at the blanket of bright lights beneath and around me, which is not unlike a piece of embroidery work bewilderingly and unrestrainedly stitched with colored threads. Since it lacks definition, it becomes intriguing. And there is no need for the visitor to look beneath the surface, as the best way to keep memories of Hong Kong alive is to keep this aerial view of the city lit up in the heart.

Time and again I tell friends that it is only logical that we are indescribable since Hong Kong is a city with an indistinct character. We are incomprehensible and even we ourselves fail to spell out who we really are. We were born and raised in this city, to which, there is the umbilical cord that connects all of us. However, we are unsure of our feelings, because there are times when we feel proud of her but there are also times when we think lowly of her. This is a knot that will never come undone, even those who have turned their backs on her are incapable of untying it.

All lost tales of Hong Kong are about a romance between this city and all of us. Together, we have been through a lot.

1992

The District of Wan Chai (I)

I am trekking across Wan Chai to run an errand early in the evening.

Southorn Playground is in an uproar. There is a mini-soccer game taking place, and both sides are well-matched. Onlookers have gathered around the pitch. Under stadium light towers, their emotions on their faces are unconcealed. Their eyes are all fixed on the players, who keep their movements swift and fast. I stay on the outer ring of the crowd. Just for a moment I am transported back to a time where the Playground looked different.

In those days, the soccer pitch was an open area. It was not enclosed by any railings, nor was it surfaced with a foundation of cement. When the sun went down, it became a street bazaar. It was a rather disorganized outdoor marketplace, but I could walk through it with my eyes closed.

Toward the northeast corner, there was the Dong-Dong-Cha – a major attraction of the night market. It was a big top, inside which street artists were performing. I never knew its proper name. "Let's go watch the Dong-Dong-Cha," Father simply said. Outside of the tent, a guy was banging a gong. DONG! DONG! CHA! After a while when the percussion sounds became monotonous, he would raise his voice to introduce the show that evening. It might be performed by a strange-looking man from the remote mountains, a pretty woman with a super-flexible body, a fire-eater, or sometimes a cock with two functioning heads. The entrance fee was ten cents. Usually the performance was disappointing. Everyone was jeering at the performer upon leaving the tent. "Don't be too demanding. It didn't cost much, did it? People are waiting outside to watch the next show. There's no need to dampen their spirits," Father said.

Right in the center of the night market, martial artists were performing kung-fu, and vendors were selling herbal medicine, pickled vegetables, or preserved fruits. It was unnecessary to defend one's territory, as it was marked by onlookers standing in a ring. Within each circle of people, a light was burning. The face of the stall owner was barely visible in the dim glow of the lamp. Martial artists usually wore a pair of black traditional Chinese pants with a white waistband. They wrapped a broad band of tired, red clothing around the hips, but had no clothes on the top half of the body. Some of them gathered the two ends of the strip of fabric encircling the waist of the pants and tied a solid square knot. As a rule, they started off beating their chests before they delivered a short speech full of clichés. Every now and then, they waved around a spear with red tassels or a big sword with a short hilt. Their performance did not interest me at all. The snack stalls were plain-looking, but they attracted my full attention. Father always bought me a dozen of dried salted plums or licorice olives for ten cents as a treat. However, watching street shows was a physically straining job. Since Father hated to see me squat on the hard ground amidst the crowd, he usually gave me a shoulder ride. Back then I was seven or eight years old, and I weighed within the average range for my age. For different reasons, both of us looked exhausted after an evening out.

A visit to Southorn Playground, which was just a block away from my childhood home, ignited excitement for the whole evening. Much as the built environment has changed over time, it is the same old place that carries the sweetest memories.

July 5, 1977

The District of Wan Chai (II)

I stroll along Hennessy Road. It is a once-familiar street that often invades my dreams, but it has changed almost beyond recognition throughout the years.

I raise my head. From a distance I let my gaze roam over the high-rises with square windows. A few walk-ups are sandwiched between them. They have seen the glories and the foibles of man, and now await their fate. The windows, tall and broad, lend an air of grandeur to the balconies on each floor. In a rapidly gentrifying city, clearing out the old (regardless of condition) to make room for the new is inevitable. I wonder why they were spared the wrecking ball in the first place.

I walk on.

My family used to live in a building. The site where it was located is two blocks away. After it was knocked down, I seldom return to this neighborhood. Most of the shops that I remember are gone, except for a camp-bed shop, a gasoline-can shop, a tailor shop that provides services for blue-collar workers, and a home appliances shop only half the space of an average-sized shop. In the past whenever I popped in, I exchanged a few pleasantries with the owners or their wives. But now they are gone too. In their place, sit idly shop assistants whose young faces I do not know. When I stop in my tracks peeping in, a couple of them cast me an inquisitive look. I am a stranger who lives in the midst of strangers.

I turn into Lockhart Road.

I walk down Jaffe Road just in time to see small pieces of ghost money thrown into the air[9] from one of the windows of a high-rise. While the old buildings are in danger of disappearing, is the world's oldest profession in danger of disappearing as well? Back in my day, as soon as someone mentioned "Wan Chai", all kinds of wild thoughts went through a foreigner's mind. It ruffled the residents' feathers, for we

[9] Translator's note: According to Chinese custom, brothel owners should offer money to ghosts before business starts every day.

prided ourselves on being decent citizens. Most of the American navy men imbibed not wisely but too well when they were in town. Much as they scared the hell out of me, the moment I heard people bad-mouth the district where I lived, I took up the cudgels for her. Only innocence dared to be so bold. It was not until a dozen years later that I realized that it was a futile effort.

Outside the shops, colored lights are brighter and neon signs are more peculiar than before. Apart from a few young women and bouncers sitting or standing outside of the bars, the street looks deserted. Most pedestrians hurry on without breaking stride. Is it too early for happy hour? Or, is business slack?

Quite honestly, I am not worried about it too much. To me, Wan Chai has become a distant memory. However, every once in a while when I pass by the streets, seeing those walk-ups immediately fills me with a warm and fuzzy feeling. Nostalgia is evoked not because one gets bored or life becomes mundane, but because one feels this intense urge to re-construct the way things were in the past. It is more than a trend.

July 12, 1977

Apropos Wan Chai

I moved from the district of Wan Chai more than two decades ago. Still, I get in a talkative mood whenever I think of her.

"7,000 US NAVY MEN SWARM ALL OVER HK" screams the headline of the newspaper. When the name of Wan Chai is mentioned, I bet all sorts of images come to the new arrivals' mind. Oh well, whatever will be, will be. Wan Chai was destined to meet her Mr. Wrong. For all I know, she had spent the past century paying a debt of love.

In the mid-19th century, the northern end of Ship Street was down on the sea-front facing Victoria Harbor. It gave a view over all ships that sailed the sea, hence its name. Looking south toward the mountains from Ship Street, one found a Hung Shing Temple erected there. It was customarily crowded with fishermen who came ashore to offer incense. Presumably there was also a Tai Wong Temple in the neighborhood, or else where did Tai Wong Street East and Tai Wong Street West get their names from? Foreign sailors landed here after their ships berthed in the dockyard. To seek spiritual consolations, they went to the Temple and recited a prayer. To indulge their carnal desires, they went to see the working girls in the vicinity of Ship Street or Stone Nullah Lane. Unlike their peers in Shek Tong Tsui (the Western District), the women did not get to serve johns who had a big heart and spent money like water. Late-night encounters only made them unclean, but did not make them rich. As soon as a business transaction was made, they were erased from their clients' memory without leaving a trace.

Ship Street was constructed before my time. What has been mentioned above is based on written records plus a pinch of imagination, which point to Wan Chai being one of the oldest red-light districts in the city.

It was this district I was born into. When I was old enough to make sense of the world, Gloucester Road was already built by reclamation. It had drastically changed the geography around the district, but nobody could have changed its destiny.

Father habitually took me for a walk down the waterfront after supper. "Let's go to the promenade," he announced while putting on his canvas shoes. We headed west on Hennessy Road and turned right onto Fleming Road. Sometimes we went one further block and walked down O'Brien Road. It was a peaceful residential neighborhood. Both streets run across Lockhart Road and Jaffe Road, except that, back then, they led straight down to the promenade. On the sea-front, shops were sparse. Wan Chai Police Station with tall doors was magnificent. Just to its right, there were a couple of storage units, which for sure did not bring much foot traffic to the whole place. After we passed by Golden City Cinema and the Gloucester Luk Kwok Hotel, we turned left onto Luard Road. Sometimes we walked as far as Fenwick Street. Both streets brought us back to Hennessy Road.

Taking a different route home gave us an entirely different impression of the district. There were night-clubs, bars, and shops that sold thingamajigs. Some shops were brightly illuminated by lights; some were not. A tattoo shop was nestled on the second floor of a residential building. Small pieces of ghost money were thrown into the air from a window of a building. An elderly woman squatted down beside a storm sewer burning joss money. Puffs of ashes flew everywhere like dancing specters. Several women, young and seductive, were touting for business in front of a bar and at the foot of a flight of stairs that led up to the apartments of a walk-up. They were deeply engaged in conversation, giggling, talking. The sight of them characteristically evoked a strange smile that started to play about Father's lips. I was old enough to know something was not quite right. I usually reacted by tightening my grip on his hand and quickening my pace in an attempt to counter-balance the pull of lustful temptations.

There was no taboo between father and daughter. In the late 1940s, I was in grade one or two, simple-minded and wide-eyed. On those evening walks, Father often told me stories from within brothels in Wan Chai and Shek Tong Tsui. In those days, working girls were referred to as "flowers" whereas the sex industry was dubbed the "scenic beauty". The euphemistic terms for indecent behavior are meant to soften the blow, but personally I find such a male thing completely unacceptable.

Father also told me agonizing stories about women living on Lockhart Road being forced into sexual slavery by soldiers during the Imperial Japanese Occupation of the city that lasted for three years and eight months. "To begin with, why was the comfort station set up in Wan Chai?" I asked. "There were other comfort stations on the Kowloon Peninsula as well," Father replied. "Still, Wan Chai could've been spared," I said. "You know, there was a navy base in Wan Chai during the Occupation. It was close to the dockyard," he said. To every question I asked, Father gave me a convincing answer. The sooner I shut up, the better.

In the 1950s, trouble was brewing worldwide. There were obvious reasons for British and United States navy vessels' frequent visits to Hong Kong. Victoria Harbor's deep, wide waters and strategic location in the Far East became instrumental in furnishing them with all kinds of supplies and services. However, there was a not-so-obvious reason for the navy men's frequent visits to Wan Chai, most of them were Americans. As soon as they landed at Fenwick Pier, sporting white uniforms in summer and blue uniforms in winter, they swarmed the streets of Wan Chai like bees or locusts. They drank, and drank themselves into stupor. They looked for fun, and had fun until they were out of their mind. Holding a Chinese woman in their arms, they believed they were the protagonist in *The World of Suzie Wong*. The motion picture stars William Holden as the white man who meets an Asian woman and loves her till the day he dies. Thanks to Nancy Kwan, who became the icon of a Chinese woman in the western countries! And thanks to Richard Mason, who created Suzie Wong!

Richard Mason was not the quintessential Hong Kong author but Huang Guliu was. In his *Biography of Ha Kau*, Huang paints a detailed picture of the red-light district in Wan Chai, which once stretched from Spring Garden Lane to Southorn Playground and was bordered by Gloucester Road.

> Ha Kau had been traipsing around all day and finally he went to the Gloucester sea-front. Auntie Luk caught his arm in a grip. She had a favor to ask him. She taught him the one survival English sentence that would allow him to conduct business smoothly in Wan Chai before she

> sent him away to talk to the half-drunken navy man on the sea-front. "Biiutifu girlo, wonai, turntyfivu dola, ok?"

Try to figure out what Ha Kau said to the navy man. It is too bad that the novelist had not used the Romanized forms of colloquial Cantonese words, or else the natural flavor of the vernacular would have been kept.

Because of the red-light district, respectable women living in Wan Chai often got hassled in the 1950s and 1960s. But there was not much they could do. Half- or completely drunken young navy men were too eager to demonstrate their sexual prowess but had no idea of how to get laid fast. They ran amok in the street. Sometimes they went so far as to enter residential buildings and bang on the door, striking so much terror into kids and women that they needed to find a place to hide. Once bitten, twice shy; I have never liked a navy man. And strange as it may seem, only the image of a navy man in white summer uniform (but not in blue winter uniform) with well-shined leather boots has remained in my memory.

Then, from some indeterminate point of time in the past onward, young navy men in uniforms have disappeared. New land was created from the sea. Harbor Road, Convention Avenue, and Expo Drive started to appear on the map. Wan Chai Tower, Convention and Exhibition Center, commercial buildings, and hotels were erected. Wan Chai has seized the place of Central District and becomes a hive of political-administrative and business activity. Surely that rankled. Central Plaza — a commercial building located in Wan Chai District but named after Central District — only symbolizes the latter's feeble effort to fight back. We know that a gilded bauhinia sculpture and a monument in commemoration of the return of Hong Kong to China are situated in Wan Chai. It was the district where the ceremonies for the handover of Hong Kong and the establishment of the Hong Kong Special Administrative Region were held. It is also the district where a flag-raising ceremony takes place every day. It seems that Wan Chai has turned over a new leaf.

I can sit back and relax, can't I?

Not yet. Seven thousands navy men from the United States have just landed. Photos printed in newspapers depict that they are in plainclothes out having fun in Wan Chai. On the sidewalk, among the women who attempt to lure them, there are Filipino faces. I wonder if pieces of ghost money are thrown out of an upstairs window in the early evening.

Wan Chai is resigned to her fate. Now hiding behind the façade of a smart, state-of-the-art commercial building, she uses illuminated, computer-controlled displays on the glass curtain walls as a cover for paying the debt of love. "VICE RETURNS TO WAN CHAI" It was a gloomy headline that appeared in an English newspaper back in 1977. I might be a worrier, but the bottom line is, Wan Chai knows exactly how to tug at my heartstrings.

P.S.:

1. I have not forgotten to solve the mystery. The survival sentence that helped Ha Kau do business in Wan Chai was: "Beautiful girl, one night, twenty-five dollars, okay?"

2. For further reading, see Carl Thurman Smith (1995), *A Sense of History: Studies in the Social and Urban History of Hong Kong*. There is a chapter about the identity of Wan Chai. A Chinese edition of the book is translated by Sung Hung Yiu.

March, 2000

For You — The Wan Chai Market Building

Although you had retired from your job, I did not ceased to drop by every now and then. I enjoyed taking a stroll down Queen's Road East before hot weather hit. Habitually, I started my walk from where you stand.

Then, one day (I forgot which day it was), it surprised me to find that you were wrapped in gigantic, square-shaped sheets of mesh material. The ends of bamboo poles were sticking out from under the cover. Obviously, the mesh material was wrapped around a bamboo cage that could not be seen from the outside. I was in a humorous mood that day. I thought that Christo and his wife, Jeanne-Claude, might have made an impulsive trip to Hong Kong. They had fallen in love with you – a seventy-two-year-old building, popularly referred to as one of the Bauhaus architectural tradition, lovingly designed by officers from the Public Works Department of the British colonial government who expressed an earnest desire to offer residents a marketplace. So, husband and wife had you carefully wrapped up, and turned you into a piece of artwork, like the Reichstag in Berlin.

It was a windy day. Standing on the sidewalk opposite you, I listened carefully. The sheets of mesh material ballooned and flapped. I could faintly hear them beating the air. Whoosh – whoosh – whoosh!

I used to believe that I really could "smell" light, because I associated light shining from your main entrance with the scent of all kinds of fresh vegetables sold by merchants inside the building. Mother usually went grocery shopping in a wet market located between Hennessy Road and Lockhart Road. It was an open-air market where covered stalls were frequented by low-income families. There were puddles of water on the sidewalk, and if I stepped on them, my pant legs would get wet and dirty. Because of the openness of the marketplace, all smells of produce faded once they came into contact with air, except for the malodor of fecal droppings that hung over the stalls where live chickens and ducks were sold. It is the kind of stink that remains poised in my memory but nothing else. However, Mother would come see you to stock up on groceries during festive seasons. Your entrance ambience was most impressive. The ceiling was high above the ground, which allowed you to hold yourself aloof from all shoppers. From the entrance, meandering flights of stairs went up to the second floor. Near the rear, there were stalls that sold live chickens. Strangely enough, the place did not reek of fecal droppings. It smelled of fresh vegetables. Back then, there were no huge metal electric fans mounted to the ceiling, but I did not feel the kind of oppressive heat that one normally experiences in a stuffy room. The smell of fresh vegetables was overwhelming. After so many years have elapsed, it is the only thing that I can call to mind when I think of you. If personality did smell, then yours would have been the smell of greens.

Years rolled by. At some point in time, you took on a new role by providing the community with leisure facilities. A friend of mine invited me to visit you and to play table tennis together. However, it was just impossible for me to imagine that there were activity rooms built under your roof. On several occasions, I had made plans to drop by but nothing panned out. I guess deep down I did not want to accept the fact that you had changed.

It is not easy to keep your body young. But it is possible — no doubt about it. However, is there any cast-iron guaranteed way to succeed in keeping the memories of a bygone era forever young?

In 2004, some enthusiasts urged that you be declared as a building of historical interest and preserved in a re-development project. I had low expectations of such an endeavor because the so-called conservation of heritage places in Hong Kong was nothing but a smokescreen. I feared a jinx. I was afraid that something catastrophically bad was going to happen, but I did not step up to the plate.

The die was cast.

On May 20, 2009, Wong Hin Yan shot a clip about you and uploaded it to YouTube. It was the first time I ever caught sight of the inside of you. In the video clip, yellow-helmeted demolition workers are milling around while the jackhammer is emitting the excruciating sound. A worker is walking on a horizontal I-beam of the skeleton frame. When interviewed, a professional remarks that the I-beam, made with high-quality steel, is probably the best of its kind. You were aging, but your stance was tough and unyielding. The sound of a jackhammer masks all other noises on the construction site. A bulldozer rolls over the ground that was laid seventy-two years ago. When my eyes rested on your scattered remains, I felt the sting of tears in my eyes.

I bet that you would have resisted it if you could.

September, 2009

A Polyptych (I): *Browsing Streets*

Interesting places in Central and Sheung Wan are like panels of a polyptych.

Walking west on Hollywood Road, one finds the charm of the Orient and the charm of East-meets-West nicely blended together on the same street. While a Caucasian is captivated by the former, a local is dazzled by the latter. This is a practical twist on two cultures that requires no academic jargon to expound on, for strolling along the street is like reading a scholarly paper.

The paint odors of a new structure linger on. The name of the building – Tian Fu (which can be literally translated as "to maximize luck") – is as graceless as it gets. Or rather, it is reminiscent of rural family history because it sounds so Chinese.

I finish browsing in a shop on the third floor (or is it the second floor?[10]), where there is an impressive array of high-quality decorative papers. Then I go down the stairs. An exhibition of the printmaking artworks by Lau Guk Zik is being staged in an art gallery. Unfortunately, I am not savvy about equipment such as the collage maker, the offset printing press, and the color printing press, nor do I know anything about painting supplies. Even so, I am bewitched by *A Window View of Hong Kong*. The lights of the city depicted in the artwork seem like distant dreams, intricate and perplexing, forceless yet profound. I am mesmerized and almost forget the world inside the quiet room. The next piece of art, *On a June Morning*, shows a different time in a different place. At first, I decide to slide my gaze away from it, but I think better of it. It

---

[10] Translator's note: There is some difference between American English and Hong Kong Cantonese in the naming of floors in a building. In Hong Kong Cantonese, the first floor is referred to as the ground floor. The floor above it is the second floor.

seems as if the artist was frustrated at the time of its production. There are traces of violence. Ghostly images wander in a state of confusion.

I take the stairs down to the semi-basement. Paintings of warm colors are hanging on a wall that subdues an excitement. It is the kind of place that evokes the Westerners' feelings of nostalgia. I crouch down and take a closer look at a small mahogany chest of drawers. The tiny drawers are ideal for storing little white jade ornaments. I pull open one of them and close it. "See if there's anything you like," a guy sitting at his desk looks up and says.

Just to see if there is anything I like, I walk over to Peel Street.

On the street, an old woman is peddling second-hand clothing and a mixed assortment of different items displayed on the ground. "For five dollars, you can choose any two of these items," she says. Weng Cheung, a spice shop that sells dried mushrooms, dried shrimps, fat choy, dried bean curd, and the like, takes up the whole sidewalk to array its merchandise. I sniff the air for the smell of pickled bamboo shoots. It is hard to describe the taste that is sour and salty, but it is all too familiar to me. Steamed fish head with pickled bamboo shoots was the most appreciated dish that only my mother and I enjoyed.

Time has left her small footprints on Pak Tsz Lane, Sam Ka Lane, Staveley Street, and Wellington Street. They are like unique notes that the city hits in a symphony.

October 24, 1994

A Polyptych (II): *Browsing Streets*

Recently I have bought a camcorder because people will only believe that something exists when they actually see it. However, I often forget to take it with me when I go browsing through the streets. (Come on, I would have to be crazy to carry a machine wherever I go.) But even if I remember to do so, I kick myself for making the purchase too late. Some of the street scenes have already vanished. For this, I always feel a pang of remorse.

I missed the opportunity to make a video of Lee Theater in Causeway Bay and the Chinese Methodist Church in Wan Chai. A while back, I was toying with the idea of making a video of the last surviving low-rise with "ready-set-trot" balconies on Lockhart Road. It was a four-story walk-up that once housed the most glamorous night-club Bar La Salle. On each floor, a hanging balcony traversed the entire length and across the front of the building. It was so deep that there was more than enough space for a horse to trot, hence its name — the "ready-set-trot" balcony. Since some young people had never seen it before, it was better to open the eye than to scratch the ear. Anyway, while I was still humming and hawing over videoing the building, it was knocked to the ground.

On Hennessy Road, there is a four-story walk-up where a pawnshop is situated. Its signboard hangs from the external walls of the building. A tall wooden screen is erected between the door and a counter with metal bars. On the wooden screen, a character inked red, which means "pawns" in Chinese, is scribed. It is meant to hide the counter from the prying eyes of passers-by and protect customers' privacy. I have only seen the inside of a pawnshop in movies, but I have never been to one before. However, it is common knowledge that the counter is typically higher than the average person. No wonder the expression goei-je, which means "to pawn" in the vernacular, can be literally translated as "to hold an object high over one's head". When I was a kid, I often worried that I was not tall enough to reach my hand up above the counter in case I needed to goei-je. One day, I could not help but confide in my mother. "You silly girl," she said, and gave me a hard stare. "There're other things you should be thinking about apart from going to a pawnshop."

For sure, videoing this pawnshop is an item on my bucket list.

A few gold jewelry shops manned by aging staff in Sham Shui Po are going to disappear anytime soon. In the past, housewives and grannies perched themselves on a stool and easily spent half a day in the shop haggling with jewelers. But people stop doing it now. Since I do not care much about accessories, I did not notice until recently that modern jewelry shops no longer have seating available.

Dai Tung, a shop on Reclamation Street that sells medicinal herbal tea with a bitter taste, will not last any longer either. Inside the shop, lights burn brightly. But the infusion has lost its leading role since the day papaya milkshakes and mango sago were included in the menu. I seldom drink it. This kind of shop becomes a rare sight in the city. Once in a while, I pass by one but I usually find it ostentatious. Two big bronze gourds, polished and shined to perfection, are installed on a counter. They are used to store the tea. It does not come cheap, though. In the past, people without means cured themselves from a heat-stroke by drinking the tea that only cost ten cents.

Videoing the gold jewelry shops in Sham Shui Po and the herbal tea shop on Reclamation Street are the next two items on my bucket list.

Authenticity cannot be faked. It is not surprising that the latest vintage-style clothing looks ridiculous in Shanghai Tang's display windows. On Lockhart Road in Wan Chai, there used to be a tailor shop that did not have front doors. Inside, a large work-table was covered with a white cloth that had turned yellowish. The tailor wore a white undershirt, hanging a measuring tape around his neck. With his job, everything just came naturally.

Shops that are not captured on video can only be replayed in my mind.

October 25, 1994

My Fond Memories of Neighborhood Stores

Shopping malls in this city become bigger and bigger. Unfortunately, they are losing their mall personalities. Some have even none.

During the festive season, the mall turns into a hub of activity center. As always, there are live performances in the middle of the entertainment venue. The whole place is packed with people, standing five deep along the railing on every floor. However, the crowd disperses as soon as the show is over. You go your way, I go mine, and we will never see each other again. I am in with the "out" crowd. I never get used to most of the mall stores that are flooded with lights shining in glorious Technicolor. With them, it is out of sight, out of mind. There is no love lost between us.

A long-time Kyoto resident, Jugaku Akiko, once described her city as "a place where the street is a platform through which people are known". Such an endearing remark speaks volumes about street etiquette from the bygone days. I enjoy browsing through the streets of an old neighborhood to meet new friends. It is a kind of human bonding, but personally, I consider it a kind of leisure activity.

The street and the mall are just as different as night and day. In the street, people meet each other. They walk through it regularly and their faces become familiar to each other over time. In the mall, people go their separate ways. They have their own reasons for going there. Some do not even have any. As soon as their business is finished, they leave the place.

Once upon a time, the streets were lined with stores — small stores in particular. They matched the owners' and their assistants' personalities. It was something you knew in the heart after you popped in a few times. Here, the owner of this store was friendly and liked to chit-chat. To do business was not a priority. You shopped often enough and you were a friend of his. Over there, the assistant of that store was meaner than a junk yard dog. The few angry words he uttered reflected badly on his image, but really, deep down he was a softie.

Small retail businesses in my childhood neighborhood had left a deep impression on me. Tim Sum, which means "sweet-heart", was a candy-store located next to Mui Fong Secondary School on Fleming Road. It was a hang-out for elementary-school kids. The owner always had broad smiles on his face, but his wife was cold and distant. Oftentimes he gave me an extra half piece when I bought butterfly cookies. Sam Yuen Noodles was located on the right side of Hong Kin Bookstore on Lockhart Road. Back then, a bowl of wonton noodles (the lingo for which is called sai-jung "regular egg-noodles") cost thirty cents. "The sour girl's here!" a wait-person would announce in a loud voice when I entered the little eatery. As the sour girl, I added five or six tablespoons of red vinegar to my bowl of noodles, and easily devoured half a jar of diced pickled cucumber. Cheung Wah Groceries was on Hennessy Road. You just phoned and placed an order for cooking oil or rice. You got your items delivered right to your door in no time. With the hospitality so characteristic of the grocer, if you stopped by the shop to get a bottle of soy sauce or some flour but accidentally ran out of money, you just paid him back later with no strings attached.

I like to browse in shops, especially those on Tai Yuen Street, Spring Garden Lane, and Cross Street in Wan Chai. Shop owners strike up a conversation with a customer effortlessly. Once I dropped into a spice shop and spent five dollars to get a pack of turmeric. The owner gave me a ten-minute lecture on how to make fried rice with turmeric and to prepare steam chicken with sand ginger. One time, I went to a roadside stall and had my watch battery replaced. The owner spotted dust on the dial. "How does it get there?" he said, and began to clean it out furiously. "There's no service charge for this. I just can't stand the sight of it."

Boutiques that sell upmarket products on the streets running east-to-west in Mid-Levels (Central) are birds of a different feather. There is one that specializes in jade ornaments and wood sculptures. It is owned by a couple. The husband is a designer-expert in wood sculptures and fine-quality jade. His wife is good at Chinese knotting. Both of them are esthetics, and they set high standards for the quality of handicrafts. At the beginning, I was just a typical browser peeking at something of interest in their shop window and that was it. Then one day, I decided to go in and check out the products. And it turned out that the three of us hit it off right away. Now I make a habit of dropping by whenever I am in the neighborhood. As usual, the husband offers me a tea before he shows me a few pieces of his pride and joy. He is the one who teaches me everything about artwork appreciation. Much as he is aware that I cannot afford to buy any of their handicrafts, he is willing to spend time with me. I am a customer in a perpetual "just-looking-around" mode, but become a favorite student of his.

In the same neighborhood, there is a well-established shop that sells preserved fruits and pickled vegetables. One day, I stuck my head in the shop. I was interested in taking a look at some vintage wrapping paper. The owner was all alone manning the counter by himself. He waved at me. "Come on in. Feel free to look around," he said. I did not buy anything, but I walked out of his shop with an old-fashioned paper shopping bag that he pressed into my hand.

Shopping malls are now springing up like mushrooms. Real estate developers have moved in. They bought up land lots in old residential areas, where shop owners go into their game as the underdogs. As tenants, they can hardly afford exorbitant rents. They are hanging from a cliff by their fingertips. And then eventually their hands have to let go. True, the government emphasizes the importance of social harmony, but what it promotes is mere rhetoric. How much does a new generation know about human bonding if all shops in the old neighborhood disappear?

March, 2008

Let's Go Watch the Sunset

"Have you ever watched the sunset in Hong Kong?" I asked a young man. He was born and raised in this city.

My question had caught him off-guard. He looked at me in amazement. "Have you?" I persisted. He knew that he could not get away. He knew that I was serious. He hung his head, contemplating my question for a while. "No, I haven't," he answered.

It did not come as a surprise, for I had not done it since a long time ago. I would have almost forgotten what it was like if I had not read Wang Anyi's essay, entitled "The Beautiful City of Hong Kong":

> The sunset in Hong Kong is incomparably unique. At first, the red giant sun is sinking unhurriedly to the bottom of the valley deep in the concrete forest. However, when it starts to descend rapidly to the abyss between two skyscrapers, for a split second, a spectacular scene presents itself. Under the canopy of the heavens, luminance shifts its evening tints and together the sun and all buildings stand still, singing songs to the tunes of anthems and dirges that flood the sky like waves. A second becomes eternity. The first star shines. The first street lamp lights up. Then, without warning, the sky darkens, and the hours of the night begin.

The young man could not believe his eyes. He shook his head. "Is it really like that? It sounds a tad arty and kind of hard to stomach," he said. "Have you ever watched a sunset framed by skyscrapers?" I persisted. "Have you ever spent five minutes watching the sun set with a quiet mind and an untroubled heart?" I persisted. "No, I haven't," he said impatiently, sort of. "Well, in that case, on what basis do you consider it a bit arty? If you're in doubt, why don't you check it out?"

Maybe, soon enough he forgets my persistent questions. Or maybe, one of these days, he will actually go and watch a sunset. Whatever he is going to do, nobody knows but himself.

What do most of the Hongkongers do in the early evening? Roads are crowded. Public transport is crammed. People quicken their steps. Just who has leisure to look up and watch the sunset? It is happy hour. The bar is dimly lit and cozy, which provides shelter for those who are not in a hurry to go home after a nerve-racking day at work. People come up with different reasons why they have never watched a sunset: "This is a metropolis. Much of the sky is obscured from view by tall buildings to resemble splinter-like pieces." "A hard life eats away peace of mind." "What to do when you live in a shoe?" And so forth.

Everybody has something to complain about. Everyone has an excuse to do or not to do something. I am not interested in finger-pointing, but if I play the blame game, I should say that it is the government's responsibility to promote quality culture education through nurturing in students the quality of being sophisticated. "What to do when you live in a shoe?" It only reveals humankind's propensity for making excuses. Aren't Paris and Tokyo big, busy cities as well? Still, Parisians and Tokyoites are refined people with refined taste. Despite cross-cultural differences, they are very similar, considering the fact that they both love nature and calmness.

The Meiji Restoration in Japan brought about industrialization and modernization. At that time, the Yamato people in metropolitan areas, known for fitting every minute into their tight schedules, went with the flow but were drowning in it. This worried educators and educationists. Consequently, they promoted the idea of spending five minutes a day to study nature and to acquire the habit of reflection. The Japanese today are totally capable of being rowdy but they also know when to quiet their mind. I believe that this is one of the benefits of education.

Introspection is the path to serenity. Only if we invite nature into the heart can we maintain introspective awareness. However, this city is raucous and busy. Our plates are always full. We get agitated. Our crowded heart needs space. We get restless. We have distanced ourselves from nature owing to the self-imposed obstacles we place in our own way in addition to obstacles represented by financial, social, and political issues.

Go catch a sunset? Maybe I am making a big deal out of nothing. But if we have reached a dead end in our attempts to find a solution, why don't we give it a try?

January, 1999

The Hills

There is daylight though it is already six in the afternoon. The weather has been humid recently. Everywhere reeks of mold and damp. This evening is a breath of fresh air, literally and figuratively. Flaming clouds return to the sky after a long absence. Now they look unfamiliar and exotic.

I lighten up as if a heavy coat has been eased off me. I stop marking my students' essays, and decide to take five in a walkway with great views of hills. The hills, lavishly covered in trees and shrubs, are most enchanting in the early hours of the morning when a gentle wind comes up with a smoldering fume. Even in the midst of winter, the view is as exciting as ever. Winds are gusting. Wild reeds are waving. Tall grass is swaying. Two towering trees with bare branches remind me of woodcut prints.

Now, under the two trees, several nonchalant stray dogs indulge in a daydream near a pile of white slatted cases. Every now and then, they lift their heads to peer at a flock of perky, chirping sparrows. My feathered friends call to mind a line from Wu Sheng's poem: "Birdsong has nothing to do with ebullience/The sun has nothing to do with brilliance." Around six-thirty in the morning, an elderly couple usually comes along the dirt path. They push a wooden cart loaded with their wares, which are as heavy as old memories of their past. Shuffling, they bend forward. They push as hard as they can toward a destination that I do not know.

During the wet season, mist hanging over the meadows in the vale below is like a quiet farmer selling foods at a marketplace. The rolling hills become as intriguing as majestic mountain ranges. I have been told that the dirt path is perfect for a late afternoon walk on a bright day. The walker is rewarded with the same kind of pleasure he can get out of a trip to the Western Hills in Beijing.

However, due to the mayhem of city life, I have not enjoyed the tranquility of the hills as much as I would like. Here and now, as I partake of a visual feast of bucolic scenery, I notice that while some trees are budding, others are still covered with droopy seed pods. The long shadows cast by the setting sun darken. All birds have returned home. The hills sit in silence, safe in the knowledge that the sun will rise tomorrow.

Speaking of budding trees, I kick myself for missing out – again – on a chance to see how new leaves mature during the growing season this year. From the moment I spotted them show their first signs of activity on a drizzly morning, I promised myself that I would check them out later on. But then I had been snowed under with work. By the time I remembered, they had already shaded everything underneath.

The hills wear a somber hue as the daylight begins to fade.

April 5, 1978

Part IV

Here comes a traveler
Under the green willow.
— Song Qi

Hidden Treasure

"You never know what you'll find when you sift through trash," Leung, my late friend, once said. And I have filed away his words in my head.

Every afternoon on my way home, I pass by a refuse collection point, where families in the neighborhood leave their unwanted items such as furniture, home appliances, brand-new wood boards, and boxes of unused ceramic tiles. Most of them are in good condition. Garbage pickers often check out the heaps of trash, and cart off whatever they find useful.

It was late afternoon that day, the sky looked pretty threatening. I quickened my pace home. The refuse collection point was crowded with several broken cupboards and cabinets. A few moving boxes were scattered haphazardly on the sidewalk, as there was no more space inside. It was a common sight. But wait! Did I just say BOXES? I never miss the chance to look for moving boxes, because they are ideal for storing books.

I opened one of them and –

Oh my, is it a dream? I had always dreamed of finding "something nice" in the trash such as out-of-print books or journals, and famous people's pictures or correspondence Deep down inside, I truly believed that a rag-and-bone man would hit the jackpot one day.

Oh my god, they're all books! Indeed, they were all books. The first one that caught my eye was the premier edition of a two-volume bestseller The Black Hero by Mong Wen published in April, 1940. I had been trying to get my hands on it for close to twenty years but all to no avail. I dug a little deeper, and found the first edition of The Fall of Hong Kong: A Diary by Sa Kongliao published in 1946. My heart was beating irregularly, my hands were shaking. I stopped digging, and looked around to make sure that the coast was clear. Then I hurried away to find a landline. I called Wai at home. I asked her to bring along a huge tote bag and a handcart, and meet me at the refuse collection point.

In the meantime, I was guarding the boxes as if they contained jewels and gems. What's inside the other boxes? Please God, I don't need rain on my field right now. Please God, you need to stop a literature-savvy guy from coming this way. In retrospect, I should have looked so comical.

The waiting time was painfully long. When Wai showed up within several minutes, we opened the boxes together. It's so dirty, yuck! It seemed that those boxes had not been opened for ages. True to type, they were hidden treasure. Wow! Wow! Working swiftly, I dumped all of their contents into the handcart. I did not care how filthy the publications were as long as they were printed in Chinese and still in one piece.

We moved quickly, pushing a full load of books on the handcart. As soon as we reached home, the first drop of rain before a heavy downpour came.

June 25, 1996

Anxiety

It was a pleasant evening. The weather was nice. We were stuffing our faces beside a food stall in the open air. "What if it starts raining?" Out of the blue, I shot a question at my friends. Worried is the one word that describes me best.

Anxiety is contagious. When I was in high school, my fellow-students referred to me as the female version of Alfred Hitchcock, because I was pretty capable of maximizing anxiety and fear.

Here is a story circulating among my co-workers. One evening, I attended a banquet in Sha Tin. After hors d'oeuvres were served, I opened my purse and dug for a few coins. A colleague thought that I was going to the ladies' room. "I didn't see any cleaner in there. There's no need to leave a tip," she said. I was mortified. "Did I tell you that I wanted to go to the toilet? When the banquet's over, I need to take a train and a cross-harbor bus to get home. I want to be sure to have the right coins ready," I said. Since then, my co-workers have started to poke fun at me. Those with a curious mind are determined to get to the bottom of it. "Seriously now, did you make it through dinner and the train trip without loosening your grip on those coins in your hand?"

The anxious disposition runs deep in my family. To be specific, Mother passed it on to me. Here is a well-remembered case.

With the peace that followed the conclusion of World War II, Hong Kong experienced an economic decline from 1945. My parents were struggling to make ends meet. Every memory I have of Mother is that of her knitting the brows. From her lips, I heard that the Civil War on the Mainland had broken out, and Gandhi's non-violent resistance in India was going on. One day, she placed a home-delivery order for sixty kilograms of rice. "World War III is coming. Remember that I had stocked up with rice before the Japs came? If I hadn't, we wouldn't have survived. Rice's a staple," she told us. From that day on, she always had rice stashed away in our house. In the blink of an eye, fifty years have passed. The trees standing on both sides of Mother's grave have reached full height, but we still have not heard the beating of a war drum. If Mother had been alive, she would have been kept on her toes for half a century. Sixty kilograms of rice would have been sitting in our house all the time.

Given that air-raid sirens went off every day in my childhood years, I have come a long way. My friends have never heard me ask: What if bombs start raining down? Come on, give me credit for it.

July 1, 1993

Our Battle Stories

1

Did Lara get me into trouble, or did I get her into trouble?

These last two months, our lives have been controlled by an invisible hand. We are completely powerless against a conquering superpower. We have been banging our head against a brick wall hunting for clues, but we are clueless.

Does that sound complicated? I haven't even started yet. But it makes perfect sense to you if you're addicted to *Tomb Raider*. It has been in the top five on the list of best-selling video games for weeks on end.

It has been two weeks since Lara was lost in a cave. She has been tested in every way. She survived a violent axe attack and bow-and-arrow assault. She fought off beasts (such as wolves, bears, and dinosaurs) lying in ambush. To cap it all, she almost drowned. As I watched her body oxygen levels on the screen going down rapidly, I found myself holding my breath nearly to the point of passing out.

Out of fear, I made her shoot blindly at any moving objects, and wasted too many bullets. Due to a mistake on my part, I forced her to jump the gun and react prematurely. Even in the dream at night, I could hear her crying out in pain when she ran into a wall. Because I hankered after every foolish vanity, I propelled her to taking multiple trips back and forth. Because I was insatiable for survival supplies and treasure, I pushed her into checking out every corner, leaving no stone unturned.

More than once, I was disconcerted by a wall standing tall in her way. At the edge of a cliff, I was undecided about whether to allow her to jump or not. I was consumed by a fear of heights, a fear of the unknown, and a fear of making life-threatening mistakes. More than once, I slowed her down. I let her round a corner warily, holding a gun with both hands ready for a shoot-out in case a monster suddenly materialized. More than once, I made her execute a flying leap, turn a somersault, or push herself into the air in an attempt to find a way out of the cave.

She is panting for breath now. Her chest is rising up and down. My fingers pause over the buttons. I am panting for breath as well. It is hard to tell if she is exhausted, as she is forever taking rapid, shallow breaths. But I am exhausted. My fingers spasm as my right hand hovers over the buttons. The constant strain on my stiff shoulders leaves me in agony. My back starts to hurt owing to prolonged sitting.

We have reached a dead end. We do not know what is going to happen. But the scariest thing is that I have lost track of time. Past, present, and future all exist at once. There is no difference between day and night. Sometimes a minute seems like an hour; sometimes an hour seems like a minute. On the screen, different images appear on a long journey, but they are produced by the same flashing colors. I do not know exactly how many hours or days have passed.

2

All along I had been flattering myself that I was the one who masterminded Lara's actions. As the fingers of my right hand moved swiftly over the buttons (there are only nine of them), she responded to my commands accordingly. Lara slowed to a walk. Lara leapt up into the air. Lara sprang forward. Lara stooped low. Lara ran with short strides … And certainly, Lara swam underwater. Needless to say, I put on my thinking cap to gain a perception of the stimulus, solve a problem, and trigger a reaction. The movements of my fingers on the buttons were controlled by the brain in my head. When I paused to contemplate my next move or work out a strategy, she would pause too, breathing hard, waiting for my instructions. When I played a prank on her or drove her crazy for kicks, she would throw herself against a wall ("Ouch! Ouch!"), or hang on the cliff with both hands, her feet moving sideways and dangling in the open air. All the while I counted myself fully in the know about the result of her effort. No one but I made the decision on speed, course, and movement.

Everything was perfect until one day I noticed a few times that the movement of her body was erratic. She even adopted a different posture. However, she did as she was told most of the time. At first, I thought I did not hit the buttons properly. I tried it a few more times but the problem persisted. In a moment of appalled recognition, I realized that she was gleefully taking her very first steps to become an independent woman.

Then, the next thing I knew, all hell broke loose when a bear appeared on the right side. I hit the button frantically and directed her to run away from it. But she defied me by running toward the bear! And when I wanted her to jump off a waterfall into water, she chose to kill herself by landing on rocks at waterside! (In due course, I will tell you how she came back to life.)

What is the force that controls her, or should I say my, actions? I break out in a cold sweat the minute this question pops up in my mind.

Both Lara and I are being manipulated by someone else.

Somewhere out there, some video game designer is full of mirth. He must be good at playing mind games too. Whenever I feel boxed in or bummed out, he offers me the right kind of encouragement to cheer me on, like a first-aid kit, a key, or a large quantity of ammunition to replenish the supply. It seems that the wolf and the bear love to play hide-and-seek. I can never predict where they come from. What lies ahead, both Lara and I do not know. What I know is that we have been manipulated by some video game designer since the game started.

November 5 – 6, 1997

A Crab Meal

I will not let this autumn pass me by without eating a crab or two. At the dinner table, friends on the same wavelength chitter-chatter while cracking a crab. I am not crazy about crab, though. It is the company that I crave.

There is a proper way to shell a crab and access the flesh inside. The task should be achieved with ease and élan. On this topic, the artist Feng Zikai had written a fascinating essay. As a matter of course, I had never seen him eat one, but his former students had. Once I was visiting Shanghai. Wenyan and his wife came by my hotel room not so much bringing me a few cooked crabs as doing a demo of how to eat a crab. And true to form, they tackled their crabs without breaking a sweat. As they indulged in chitchat, they snapped each joint of the leg with confidence, and then pulled out the flesh in one go.

Even if I had learned something from them, I would not have had any chance to practice the skill. I have a crab meal only once or twice a year. And it can be a messy undertaking. I shovel everything into the mouth without extracting the flesh out of the shell first. Since the flesh is super-glued inside the hard shell, I have to spit out the shell after a few chews. Naturally, I am not eating well. The flesh stuck to the shell just keeps piling up, and eventually forms a small mound on the table. To top it all off, my fingers often get poked by the jagged shell. I am just a hopeless crab-eater.

I prefer to invite friends over rather than dine out. A weekend dinner allows us to linger over wine and crab, as there is no need to get up early for work the next day. I do not mind if my house guests drink, although people who dominate the conversation or get aggressive after a few drinks certainly break up the party. We carry on good, long talks. We segue in conversation, changing the topic from literature to world affairs so smoothly that none of us even notice. Usually I am a good listener. I join in the laughter, but speak few words. That is all I want.

Some people take pride in their skill of eating a crab. They take the hard shell apart, get every last morsel of flesh out of it, and then re-assemble the shell. But I think it just spoils the fun. And politics is one subject that dampens the mood at a crab meal in much the same way.

I can live without crab, but my desire to meet up with friends over crab has become intense over recent years. Oh well, many kiss the child for the nurse's sake.

October 28, 1993

Moss

Moss knows the way to my heart.

I have six planters of mosses. The pots are of different shapes and different materials. There are square and round pots. And there are white ceramic pots, red clay pots, and porcelain pots with under-glaze blue. All of them are filled with artificial soil mixes, which support different species of mosses I collected from different places.

The weather has been warm and humid of late. The roadside buttress wall is almost overnight covered with moss. Over the past few years, I had meant to flex my green thumb but nothing came out as planned. At the beginning of this year, I was saddled with work. Yet, I was determined to give it a shot. Wasn't it strange that while I was complaining about a busy work life, I decided to take up container gardening as a new hobby? Please read on.

A little while ago in spring, I got edgy only too often when the hectic schedule I kept smoldered like fire. I was conscious of the fact that restlessness could wreak havoc not only on my body but also on my personal relationships with other people. However, many a time I let people get under my skin. It was only in hindsight that I realized what indeed an impatient person I was.

One day, a light rain fell when I was on my way home. It sprinkled over a smooth carpet of green moss that hugged the ground under a tree. I opened my umbrella, and watched. I was mesmerized for a moment. Miraculously, I felt serene. My heart was as calm as a millpond.

Moss characteristically manifests timeless elegance. "Regardless of how little or how much time you have, spend a quiet moment looking at a luxuriant growth of moss every now and then. It helps you achieve a peaceful state of mind where action and awareness are merged. You can shut out everything around you other than undisturbed tranquility. Once you stay focused, you won't feel like yakking non-stop at the top of your voice. Just sit quietly, or stand at the railings. You simply forget what you've wanted to say," my mentor once said. I have no doubt he spoke the truth, as I will never forget the sense of serenity I felt the day I visited Koke-dera, the moss temple, in Kyoto.

Container gardens are close-up delights, which are ideal for adding a luscious green look to my house. And moss is preferable to other plants. While a seemingly infinite stretch of mosses in a garden teaches me the meaning of life like a philosopher, those grow in a tiny pot less than two inches in diameter charm me with an easy grace.

Every day after work, I spend a few refreshing moments gazing at the planters in silence. Once my soul is quiet and stress is soothed, I sit at the desk. In the wash of ambient light from a table lamp, I begin marking my students' assignments.

April 19, 1978

To Sir with Love

I never let readers get a glimpse of my former self: one who was young, vulnerable, and ignorant. I was bungling all the time. However, I will pull out all the stops to honor the memory of Professor Tang Junyi's life and attest to his mentorship (in case you did not get a chance to meet him). I am ready to tell three of my stories here. It requires a great deal of soul-searching, though.

It was my first year in junior high when all hell broke loose. I had always been my parents' baby and favorite child. But over the course of the next two years, first I was stunned by the sudden loss of my mother, then I was shocked by my father's late-life re-marriage, and finally I was devastated following his unexpected demise. To top it off, I was shaken by his young, new wife's hostility. There was so much pain and suffering in the world and it was just all piling up on me. I was mad at God for treating me unfairly. I was consumed with rage. I became bitter and resentful. For four years, I was reclusive. I locked myself in my poorly lit bedroom located in the middle of an apartment. It was my childhood home once filled with joy and laughter. Memories flooded back and reclaimed my mind. I did not eat well, so my health declined. I allowed myself to be taken advantage of by a tenant who rented a spare room in my home. Day by day, I grew addicted to creating self-inflicted drama.

It was a turbulent year when I got promoted to grade nine. Like all young people my age, I was full of myself and averse to the society of others. I was an angry adolescent undergoing a change that I could not have anticipated. Thankfully, my appetite for reading whetted by my mother did not weaken. When I had finished my homework, I would wander through the streets aimlessly, or I would hole up and read a book. The summer of that year was a crucial turning point. As luck would have it, I met Professor Mo Kefei, who held a part-time position at New Asia College. (He was one of my mentors, but sadly, he was gone at the time of writing.) Under his intellectual guidance, I performed a systematic study of academic literature. I was also given a copy of *Experiences of Life* written by Professor Tang, which is, in my opinion, a very important book to read.

In the evenings, I buried myself in Professor's Tang book, as a lamp cast its beam onto page after page of texts that revealed extraordinary foresight. I felt that reading his book was a real milestone on the journey of my life.

When I was sad, he said, "When heartfelt sadness comes, welcome it into your arms. Sadness from the bottom of your heart removes all psychic debris and cleanses your soul. The lake and the mountains bathing in rain are more charming. Likewise, the world you see through tearful eyes is more enticing."

When I was untrusting, he said, "Do not be cynical unless you have confirmed evidence against others. It is a great sin to accuse somebody of an act he did not do. Only when you select a lens with correct focal length do you see the good in others."

When I was feeling tired and lethargic, he said, "Excel yourself if you believe in beliefs. Your hard work is allowing you to open up new avenues for yourself. By the sweat of your brow, you learn to enjoy the process not just the outcome."

In addition, I was encouraged to pursue an eclectic range of interests. He said, "You will not be distracted when you are attracted to many different pursuits, because your heart is comparable to a silver moon that shines on hundreds of lakes. A sensible life is a tapestry made by tightly interweaving different kinds of experiences. It helps you grow as a person."

I had been an angry and bitter teenager at rock bottom until I read Professor Tang's book. I began to breathe easier. I started thinking sensibly. I endeavored to act up to Professor Tang's instructions. I was hoping to steal a glance at the silvery moonlight breaking through the clouds after the rain and illuminating the entirely new world.

Driven by my passion for his philosophy, I decided to become his student. I set myself a goal of getting into New Asia College. Yet, money was an issue. In an effort to clinch a scholarship, I nearly killed myself acing the final school-leaving examination. Then, I had to pass a college interview.

The faculty member who conducted the college interview was Professor Tang, during which he asked several general questions. Today, I do not remember the answers I gave him except the last one.

"Do you have a passion for Chinese culture? Do you believe that it can thrive in Hong Kong?" he asked. It was very likely that he had read my admission application. I was asked to rank my choices of college in order of preference, but in all the six boxes provided, I wrote down the same institution, which was New Asia College.

My answer to his first sub-question was positive, as I had always taken a keen interest in Chinese culture. As for the second, I blundered. I was born and raised in this city. And then I went to public schools. "It's a hopeless situation," I replied guilelessly.

He lifted his head in incredulity, and that look of pity I saw in his eyes remains memorable to this day. And that was where the interview ended, since there were no further questions. Later, my friends and I compared notes. They made a mountain out of a molehill. They felt that my response to the last question was unsatisfactory and speculated that I might not get admitted. It turned out that the stars were all lined up. I got into New Asia.

The summer sun brightened up the morning. The grand windowpanes were tinted a shade of sky-blue. Standing in the library, I was awestruck by the boundless sea of knowledge. I used to think that I was better than everyone and anyone else in the class, but now my arrogance was shattered into pieces. Student life, the degree program, and different modes of teaching generated both excitement and anxiety. As a freshman who enrolled in the Introduction to Philosophy course, I found it particularly stress-inducing to try to jot down every word I heard during Professor Tang's lectures in the first month.

Later that year, something happened. In New Asia, it was customary for boarders to fly the "national" flag on campus in October. But things were about to change, because the college had become a constituent of a tertiary institution funded by the British government. All freshmen were utterly confused about what was happening. But one thing was clear: senior students were obviously upset. At a rally, for the first time in my life, I saw so many people shed tears for the country we knew. And also for the first time in my life, I heard Professor Tang address politically sensitive issues regarding Chinese people, culture, and moral principles.

All of a sudden, my personal problems seemed unimportant, as I realized the insignificance of my own self against the scale of the universe. From that time on, I had tapped into something larger than myself.

During my four years in New Asia, I took numerous courses taught by Professor Tang. It is truly hard to describe with examples how he had influenced my thinking and behavior. A gentle wind brings nature to life in spring, but no one can catch it and show it to others: "Look, this is a breeze." I never went to see him in his office. Still, I had learned and grown so much from his publications and lectures. Those who had watched him in action recalled that he totally absorbed himself in teaching, oblivious to the world around him. The way he taught a class was testimony to what he said, "Education can be defined as the selfless, responsible cultivation of learning. It is the noblest and best deed of all." True to form, his lectures were represented in a two-fold aspect: to impart knowledge by means of language; and to command respect through his personality. I was absolutely captivated by the latter.

I was by no means a learned woman after spending four years in college. However, I had reached a higher level of consciousness: "In the vastness of this world, my aspirations stand loftily/Witnessed by the deep sea, the high heavens, and the infinite end of eternity."

Upon graduation from New Asia, I went to a teacher-training institute. I was formally qualified when I entered the teaching profession with passion and conviction. However, the journey that I had embarked on was a long one. I struggled to realize Professor Tang's deeply held beliefs. "If we examine the character of a child, we see that every child has the potential to become a respectable person." At that time, I was a young woman, very green and immature. I forgot that he also said, "It is highly possible that a child develops all of his bad character traits but none of his good ones. Teaching is like holding a child's hand while navigating along a cliff edge. A teacher always finds himself on thin ice throughout his entire career. There is not a day when he can sit back and relax." Nor did I think of the fact that our society was undergoing rapid change. Professional ethics were under pressure. Consequently, obstacles that I had encountered set me back. My courage wavered. I felt wretched.

In my seventh year of teaching, serious doubts gnawed at me when two adolescent girls from my class had fallen victim to temptation. Disaster struck. They got into trouble in spite of all my efforts. Listening to their words of remorse, I was appalled. I felt like a rescue crew member whose heart skipped a beat. They had trusted me, and I was able to tighten my hold on them. Yet somehow, they slipped from my hands and dropped into a huge abyss. Overwhelmed by a sense of helplessness and sadness, I wanted to ask Professor Tang for advice. However, every time when we met, I was so engrossed in his words that I forgot about the reason for my visit. And surprisingly, what he said always had direct relevance to me, as if he knew why I went to see him in the first place.

One day, he said to me, "You look frail. You can use a career break as an opportunity to reflect on anything that has been troubling you. And then you'll see if what you believe is an illusion." He recommended me for a fellowship to do research at Kyoto University in Japan just like that.

I left my job and spent an uneventful, idyllic year in Kyoto. The distance helped to put things back into perspective. I became aware of the umbilical cord between my own self and my city. There was not a day that went by that I did not think about my school and my students. In a state of inner harmony, I knew with absolute clarity what I wanted. At long last, I had found the place where my heart belongs.

That summer, Professor Tang passed through Kyoto. It gave him the opportunity to take me to Nanzen-ji Temple. We sat cross-legged on red mats. Our eyes roamed over the luster of green grass grown in the courtyard. While I was sampling unseasoned Yu-Tofu, he quoted from Shi Zhenlin, "Lack of intensity is delightful, but lack of mildness is upsetting." Instantly, my focus was refreshed like a land washed clean by the rain. I oriented myself and walked down the path I had chosen on my life journey.

There are people who admire Professor Tang because he was a "scholar"; a "philosopher"; a "gentleman". But there are also people who regard him with contempt because he was "muddle-headed"; "stubborn"; "unconcerned with which way the wind blows". How do I describe him as a person when I introduce him to the younger generation? Much as I may not have known him well enough to venture an opinion, I should be happy to say that he was a doer; a man of principle; and a guardian angel of mine.

Under the night sky, the calm water extends tens of thousands of miles. As the waves are rippling, the reflection of bright moonlight is transformed into silvery stardust like sparkling sprinkles. There is no denying that unless he is blind, one who stands high enough sees it all.

March 15, 1978

Like Teacher, Like Student

Color me old-school, or call me a die-hard, I always find the bonding between teacher and student, or should I say kung-fu master and apprentice, most heart-warming. Funnily enough, my understanding of this particular bonding has nothing to do with any education theory or my teaching experiences. In fact, it is deeply affected by novels and movies of the martial arts genre, ranging from old-time radio drama stories about Shaolin heroes like Fong Sai Yuk and Hu Huiqian to motion pictures directed by Zhang Che, Lau Kar Leung, Jackie Chan, and Sammo Hung.

Talk about the kung-fu master! Naturally, he is a martial arts expert. He usually hides his light under a bushel. And only a poker-faced or eccentric man conforms to the stereotype of a kung-fu master. In some way, he considers himself above the law. He is not particularly kind or patient with the apprentice. He seemingly provides no guidance for the apprentice. Surely there is no curriculum designed for any training classes. Right from day one, the master uses every opportunity to torture the apprentice. Compared to being hung upside down under the sun, or doing deep knee-bends while balancing a water receptacle on top of the head, it is just duck soup to go gathering wood in mountainous areas, or start a fire in a wood stove. Of course, none of these help to hone the apprentice's kung-fu skills. The master is so unpredictable that the apprentice often feels pushed to the point of quitting. However, a listener tuning in to the radio or a viewer sitting in a cinema needs not worry. As the story goes, several years later, one day, the master decides to teach the apprentice a set of most powerful techniques that he has spent the whole life developing. He passes on what he prizes like a legacy, and does not hold back on it. Aha, everything is so crystal clear now! The "maltreatment" he gave the apprentice turns out to be basic training! It was also a way to see if the apprentice is capable of enduring hardship and willing to comply with an order.

As for the apprentice, well, he may be sort of cocky, or his head is mixed up in the beginning of the story. But then later, he is truly impressed with the master, who is one giant of a man, as far as his martial arts skills are concerned. At first, he pleads with the kung-fu master to take him on, but does not succeed. However, his mind is made up and he will not take no for an answer. At long last, the master relents. The apprentice puts his shoulder to the wheel, and grits his teeth without complaining. He seems to be able to tolerate any kind of behavior from the offbeat master, who is erratic in treating him, and whose words are often too harsh. In the end, the apprentice learns from the master all the unbeatable fighting skills! And ever after the master and the apprentice become one heart, and one mind, tra-la! Even if they are separated in flesh, they are inseparable in spirit!

My reflections on the bonding between teacher and student are also grounded on the true stories from the *Analects* and the *Holy Bible*. Confucius and Jesus were similar in many ways. Both of them were teachers who did not adapt any specific pedagogical model. Apparently, their lessons extended well beyond the classroom walls. While Confucius taught moral studies, civic studies, and classics, Jesus had much wisdom to impart on the subjects of how to love humanity and gain eternal life. The curriculum (if there was one) that they came up with lay in the fuzzy middle in a spectrum from abstract to concrete, because the nature of their teachings was primarily based on a particular conception of the real world. A significant number of people were interested in their doctrines, but Confucius only had seventy-two highly committed disciples, and Jesus, twelve. Regrettably, Yan Hui, the favorite of Confucius, died young, whereas Judas betrayed Jesus with a kiss.

As preachers and doers, Confucius and Jesus had both left their marks on history. Throughout their lives, they had forged a bond with their disciples, which I always find fascinating. Their disciples wandered the world with them through good times and bad times. And they did that of their own free will. The preachers and their disciples lived together in reduced circumstances. And there is no better way for one person to read another than living together under the same roof. Despite their little imperfections in the character, both preachers remained well-respected by their disciples. Constant company and over-familiarity did not diminish the disciples' admiration for them, because they taught the goodness of the heart through action, and their behavior was worth emulating.

As experienced preachers, they had clear thoughts on the strengths and weaknesses of every disciple. For that reason, they were capable of helping each of their disciples realize his full potential. On one occasion, Confucius fully endorsed everything Zeng Dian said, but on another occasion, he rebuked Zai Yu for dozing off during the day (he compared him to a piece of inferior wood discarded by a carver). Jesus earnestly encouraged his disciples to do good works and let their light shine. But, in a completely unsubtle way, he had forewarned Peter of his three acts of denial. Words simply cannot describe the kind of relationship between the two preachers and their disciples, which included giving and receiving, mutual understanding, interactions, patience and tolerance, transmission and reception of knowledge, and so forth.

Out on a boat, or up on a hill, both Confucius and Jesus were tempted in every way. Both had been hit with a profound power of loneliness and despondency. Their disciples had left everything behind to follow them. In pursuit of truth, there was certainly a price to pay, but their hands were not idle, because their purpose of life was sacrifice and service. Both preachers and their disciples worked together in a spirit of partnership that was based on mutual caring. And I find it deeply touching.

June, 1991

The Spirit of *Red Beard*

To To and I met up the other day. I fell into a reverie as soon as he geared the conversation toward Mifune Toshiro and – naturally – Kurosawa Akira. Mifune and Kurosawa worked together on *Red Beard* (Akahige). It was a film from which I drew much inspiration for mentoring my students many years ago.

Red Beard is a 1965 Japanese film on release in Hong Kong sometime between 1966 and 1967, when I first entered the teaching profession. In those days, kids were more manageable and better behaved. However, every pig had his St. Martin's Day coming to him. As a young novice teacher, I was having problems with some difficult students. The more I submerged myself in my job, the more they dampened my enthusiasm. Obviously, I did not reap what I sowed. I was disappointed. Worse still, my students and I frequently got our signals crossed. I found myself in an undesirable position a little too often. In the end, I worked myself into the ground. I felt deflated.

I'm doomed at the outset! An alarm bell went off in my head! I had got a long career ahead of me. I needed to do something to help myself feel better. Otherwise, I should consider changing lanes, or joining the wily old birds club established by co-workers who became jaded after holding on to their job too long. I was inexperienced. I decided to get advice, but did not know whom I could turn to. The teacher-training college I went to did not prepare me sufficiently for the psychological crisis that I had been facing. I truly loved teaching, honest to God! I was reluctant to throw in the towel just because some students of mine bit the hand that fed them. What am I going to do? I asked myself day in and day out.

As if on cue, the film *Red Beard* directed by Kurosawa and starring Mifune opened in Hong Kong. In the film, there was a most memorable scene that inspired me beyond belief. The true meaning behind it buoyed me up like a ring-buoy, and, in turn, saved my career. Trusting that it would help me explore my psyche, I bought a DVD of it lest it would not be seen again on a cinema screen. From then on, that scene never fails to remind me what is important in teaching. Whenever my hand gets bitten, I conjure up the image of Dr. Niide Kyojo played by Mifune. I know it sounds melodramatic now, but it is entirely true.

Dr. Niide is a tyrannical medical practitioner. He always keeps a straight face. As a matter of fact, he looks more like a pirate than a consultant who provides training for junior physicians. One day, he rescues an ailing teenage girl from a brothel, and assigns her to a fresh-faced doctor as his patient. Day and night, the caring young man looks after her. However, the girl is wary. She always eyes him in hostile silence. Whenever he gives her medication, she pushes the spoon away from her mouth with so much force that he spills the liquid. While Dr. Niide looks on, the same thing happens over and over again. She never relaxes her antagonistic stance, and finally the young doctor sinks into deep despondency.

Without a word, the veteran of the clinic takes the spoon. He crouches down facing the girl. A wide, sunny smile splits his thuggish face. This is definitely a first for him! (Wow, Mifune is brilliant! There is a gentleness about him that belies his stormy countenance. The viewer simply forgets that up to that moment in the story, Dr. Niide has been rude and unfeeling toward his colleagues.) Unfortunately, the girl does not appreciate his effort. Again and again, she shoves away the spoon. But again and again, he lifts the spoon, and brings it to her mouth. The whole time, he cocks his head, his smile warming. Cautiously, the frightened girl mirrors his posture, and cocks her head too. She looks at him, and again, she pushes his spoon away, although less forcibly but more tentatively than before. Now, her hostility begins to melt. When his spoon touches her lips once more, she opens her mouth, and takes her first spoonful of medication. It is for her damaged body – and for her injured heart as well.

I have given a blow-by-blow account of the scene, like, how the girl brushes away Dr. Niide's hand, and how hell-bent he is on feeding her medication. Thirty years ago, it had aroused my intense interest in teaching, and since then, I have been in the grip of Akahige fever. My body temperature never goes down.

April 1, 1998

The Silver Moon - In Respectful Memory of Yamtse[11]

She had been the Hong Kong icon of Cantonese opera famous for her cross-gender acting performances. She had been the silver moon shining on a still earth. But now she is gone. All that is left is nothing but our memories of her, frozen in a mirror that defies time and endures beyond the bounds of mortality.

Clothed with an aura of sophistication, Yamtse had taken on many male roles of an ancient scholar. On stage, "he" was like a brilliant polar-white star, or the brightest orb of night. "He" was absurdly, obsessively fascinated with "his" love. "He" stole a peek at her through willow branches in a boat. "He" smashed a zither in a fury upon hearing the news of her wedding. "He" had an encounter with her under a plum blossom tree. "He" started a writing project on the subject of springtime outing but aborted it when visited by "his" dead lover's spirit. Occasionally "he" was conversationally playful, which made "his" love half-pleased, half-offended. As always, "he" was electric, magnetic, and charismatic in "his" own unique way, in circumstances where "he" was a victim of terror bullied by the most powerful people, or a lost soul dogged by unexpected misfortune.

"He" waved "his" wide sleeves and moved "his" fingers with effortless grace comparable to that of the man of letters who lived in another time, in another world. The audience was mesmerized. Her very existence was like an otherworldly touch added to a Realist painting. In the picture, there were no rugged rocks and stinking waters. There were

---

[11] Author's note: "Yamtse" was a term of address that conveyed esteem in addressing or referring to Ms. Yam Kim Fai, a Cantonese opera artist in Hong Kong. She died on November 29, 1989. This essay is dedicated to her. It will be placed on the altar at her funeral.

only green mountains and babbling streams in a land far away from human settlements.

What did Imperial China look like? And what did a young man of letters in Imperial China look like? The responses to these questions would have been tediously long in speaking or writing. Fortunately Yamtse was the answer. She had donned many roles of a young scholar. When the stage of the theater was illuminated by spotlights, "his" story came alive. "His" tears and laughter, as well as "his" yearning for and devotion to "his" love, had touched a chord with the audience in the seating area. Watching her in action was one of the transcendent moments in our lives. Everything was etched in our memory, but nothing would be preying on our mind when the curtains were brought down.

Yamtse was well-known for her portrayal of a tender and caring man with an appropriate measure of a devil-may-care attitude. Acting blithely unconcerned is not as easy as you think. "He" might be trustworthy and clever, but "he" also needed to have a little guile. (If she had gone overboard, "he" would have been a cunning man.) That was the reason why "he" made "his" lover half-pleased, half-offended. The tale of "his" love story was a breeze on a moonlit night in today's world, where the landscape is not so pretty.

People of my generation are grateful to Yamtse for adding an otherworldly touch to the real world. Now she is gone, and an era of romance has come to an end. "I have seen all the living under the sun throng to the side of the second lad who replaces him [the old king]." Is that what is going to happen? Will we ever find someone to replace her? We had been in love with her, but our silver moon is now and forever frozen in the mirror of memory. We are all by ourselves.

December 5, 1989

The Hats and Costumes from another Era

On a few occasions, I admired them on display in pristine windows: the phoenix crown, the jeweled helmet, the red robe embroidered with golden thread, and the two-piece blouse and skirt set. And on a few other occasions, I stood even close enough to reach out and feel my fingertips rubbing against them.

Thirty-eight years ago, they were tailor-made for two renowned Cantonese opera performers in Hong Kong[12]. When I saw them on stage at that time, other things had diverted my attention away from them. The stage was lit by spotlights. Songs were being sung. Dances were performed. All kinds of colors were dazzling to the eyes. The music was ever so pleasing. The stage clothes just could not catch my eye.

Almost four decades later, the young protégées of the two renowned performers decided to bring the classic, *The Flower Princess*, back to the stage. New costumes for the whole troupe were specially acquired in Beijing, Suzhou, and Hangzhou, where tailorship is renowned for its sublime quality. However, before the opera opened, there had been moments that caused the protégées to ponder if they should take the opportunity to bring their sifu's old stage clothes back to life. Should they be seen alongside the brand-new ones on stage, where glitz and glitter were produced by modern stage lighting? Would wear and tear cause them to pale into insignificance? Those were the worries that could not be easily warded off.

On the opera premiere evening, when the curtains were drawn open, the newly acquired glamorous costumes of vibrant colors that featured exquisite embroidery appeared on stage. Yet, who else but god could have known that the two protagonists swapped their costumes for the

[12] Translator's note: They were Yam Kim Fai and Bak Sheut Sin.

vintage clothing that their sifu wore thirty-eight years ago when the performance reached the penultimate scene?! In the last two scenes ("A Memorial to the Throne" and "Death of Fragrance"), the age-old items stole the new garments' thunder. The recent acquisitions, albeit extravagantly lavish, were too flashy. They paled in comparison with the old ones all at once.

An old Pekingese tailor once gently stroked those costumes from another era. "It's so delicate, so delicate," he kept saying, with admiration written all over his face. "It's perfection, eh, it's perfection," he sighed. "These days it's impossible to get top-quality sewing materials. The master tailor no longer exists," he continued. His tone turned sad. "No matter how much money you're willing to spend, there's no way you can have something like this. Imitations might look similar enough, but they just can't hold a candle to them," he said almost apologetically. The honest man was ashamed of himself.

His complaint about the quality of sewing materials makes sense to me. In those days, golden embroidery thread was finer and smoother. It keeps the corners and edges of each shape well-defined when light plays on the design. Since it has an unpretentious appearance of subdued luster, it glimmers but does not give a superficial impression of brilliance. And silk and satin were softer and sleeker. They were light as mist without weight. Think of a satin robe if you want a snug option to wrap up in. It drapes over the body and hugs it like a second skin. Whether you wave the loose sleeve, or make the slightest movement to part the long side slit, it reflects light – and there is a translucency that gives a whirl to the reflection. It is indescribably charming.

The tailor's complaint about workmanship also makes sense. In those days, tailors had developed consummate skill in the handicraft. Their lively fingers danced around on a piece of fabric, literally and figuratively. In *A Study of Embroidery*, Chen Dingpei gives a set of must-have criteria for determining the best embroidery work, namely uniformity, tension, perpendicularity, harmony, thickness, evenness, and density. Take a closer look at those vintage pieces of costumes. They have surely met all of the essential criteria for the highest-quality work. "There is uniformity in making stitches and creating well-defined patterns, which results in aesthetic appeal." "Uniformity and tension have a cause-and-effect relationship. Starts and stops have even tension and blend in uniformly with other stitches." "There is a balance to the design if it is stitched on the grain line of fabric. The design should look perfectly and naturally balanced like the unwrinkled surface of a rivulet in spring. Fabric grain lines are perpendicular, as straight as the string of a musical instrument which is capable of playing songs at different tempos." "There is a harmony among the objects in the design unless the design is meant to be stitched on a slant. If the design is stitched on a slant by mistake, starts and stops do not have even tension. By 'harmony', it means symmetry in breadth and density." "An all-over raised pattern on the fabric should not pucker around the edges. Look horizontally across the surface to check for lumps." "Keep a nice even tension throughout, for a single mistake can ruin everything you have worked for... Advance slowly and tortuously until the job is done." "Short stitches are an open sesame to the high-quality work. The higher the stitch count, the lower the risk of puckering. The shorter the stitch length, the higher the density of the embroidery design." These are words of wisdom. But if you want to get a piece of item that meets all of these requirements, well, you are crying for the moon.

As I sat in the audience, I fixed my gaze on the long flowing red robe with embroidery patterns gleaming with golden thread. It was flying through the air and seemed to have acquired a life of its own. I was beguiled. The subtleness of the coloration and exceptional harmony of the design were most enticing. "Included in the patterns, there are a hundred stunning mountains and hills, as well as a thousand imposing ridges and cliffs." I delighted myself with the sight of it and was inebriated with immense pleasure. I could not believe that it was the very same robe that had escaped my notice thirty-eight years ago.

July 1, 2007

The Red Capital City under High Clouds

In September, 1921, Qu Qiubai, a.k.a. the "Young Man from the East", arrived in Moscow. It was a starving city thousands of miles away from the political pilgrim's homeland. During his stay in the capital, he fell ill due to the brutal cold weather. He had written several poems and essays about his unpleasant experience under a collective title "A Moon in the Eastern Sky". For example,

> I embarked on a longish journey,
> To a country hungry and snowy.
> People say: the first snows come in August,
> But it is merely hearsay off target.
> In the autumn air there's a chill,
> Bitter coldness's forever frozen still.
> Over the red capital high clouds fly,
> They cover a moon in the eastern sky.

He opined, "People in Moscow suffer extreme deprivation. I think I'd be better off if I returned home."

***

In August, 1987, I arrived at the airport in Moscow. It was nearing nine o'clock in the evening by the time my travel companions and I took a tourist coach to the downtown area, which is not far away from Red Square. The major streets that ran through the city were lined with massive buildings in somber silence. They were unimaginably huge, bathed by the sun in a shock of bright light. When chilly breezes came up, I draped a sweater over the shoulders. There I stood in the street watching the world go by.

The first snows did not come in August, nor was there any moon in the eastern sky. It had been sixty long years since Qu wrote Pilgrimage to the Red Capital – God rest his soul.

The appearance of our hotel was as imposing as all other buildings, except that its many-windowed façade that lacked the stone color produced a less forbidding style. While some of my friends grumbled about certain facilities of their rooms, I remembered what Qu's room was like:

> My room is well-equipped. There are a desk, a chair, a bed, and an electric light… It shows that the road to socialism is paved by capitalism.

I opened the two-layered windows, and was gratified to find that the streets were still in bright sunlight. A cool flurry of air drifted through the windows. *Let's go for a walk*, I suggested.

Gorky Street was extraordinarily straight and wide.

It was about nine o'clock in the evening. There was no warmth left in the splendid sun, and yet its beams were full-dazzling. Red Square and St. Basil's Cathedral are just a stone's throw away. The buildings looked surreal, like something out of a fairy tale, as the sunset shone a golden light through them.

The Moscow Hotel and The Intercontinental Hotel are elegant and magnificent. Both of their front door entryways are disproportionately small to the enormous size of the buildings. Inside, a couple of burly doormen dutifully stood guard. The glass entry doors remained firmly shut. A written notice read: "PLEASE PRODUCE PROOF OF REGISTRATION UPON ENTRY". It successfully drew a hard-and-fast line between indoor and outdoor spaces.

The sidewalks were bustling with people who lived their metropolitan lives. Some pedestrians were eating super-sized ice-cream. Tourists must visit places such as Red Square and the Museum. However, there were several things about this city that only foreigners noticed.

In the street that was lined with shops, people wearing summer clothes, trench coats, or even fully-lined overcoats formed an orderly queue. It was their daily routine. They first waited in a line to browse through a shop looking at the merchandise that was available that day. Then, they went to another line and waited to pay for what they were going to buy. And finally, they lined up again to pick up what they had bought.

I caught sight of a sharply dressed man. He had just bought some tomatoes that looked puckered and wrinkled. He had his briefcase open. And then, one by one, he gingerly placed the tomatoes into it. When our eyes met, I was apologetic for failing to play the role of a polite tourist. Still, I found it hard to tear my gaze away from his tomatoes and caring hands.

That suddenly reminded me of something. I had not seen any black bread over the past few days. Qu wrote,

> At first glance, one sees black bread as something that presents demonstrable facts about the country. But upon close scrutiny, it has its worth. It is just that it takes so much mental effort to see through it. All theories in socialist classics seem unchallenging by comparison.

When he sampled its flavor for the first time, he commented, "It tasted bitter and sour, and produced earthy, stinky smells. The Chinese have never tried it. It's absolutely unbelievable!" Needless to say, he recounted how difficult it was to buy daily necessities even though he had money.

Oh well…forget it, I said to myself, it was sixty years ago.

2

There was a knock on the door when I was about to go to bed. I opened the door to find a big woman standing right outside. She was the room service and housekeeping staffer on the floor I was staying. She tiptoed into my room, and turned to close the door. A strange smile broke into her face.

I was alarmed. I thought she was executing a search warrant in a police investigation, but then she started rambling in Russian. Of course, I did not understand her. Fortunately, body language transcended culture. She finally managed to get her message across – she wanted cosmetics and clothes. "Ruble, ruble," she kept saying the one word I understood while rubbing the thumb against the index finger frantically. My educated guess was that she could pay me in rubles. I shook my head and opened the door. She had no choice but to leave.

There were also other things I could not forget, like the happy face of my friend who sold her personal belongings for a good price; the story of a travel partner who sold her used plastic water-bottle for ten rubles; and the imploring eyes of an elderly porter who hung back at the door after carrying luggage to my hotel room. "Souvenir, souvenir, cigarette, cigarette," he said in broken English.

More than half a century ago, Qu wrote,

> A vehicle pulled up alongside our coach. Several soldiers used gestures to tell us that they wanted a smoke… The driver climbed into our coach to say goodbye. They were on their way back to Chita. They would like to have some cigarettes. 'Horrible! Horrible! … Life's hard!' he said.

I had no idea of how Qu felt at that moment, but I had a heavy heart when I shut the door upon the elderly porter.

3

Naturally, as a tourist, I did not miss Moscow's Exhibition of Achievements of the National Economy.

Inside the Space Pavilion, my group of visitors meekly followed a tour guide. She was a no-nonsense woman. She had a confident tone of voice bursting with national pride. She expounded at length on the information about the world's first artificial satellite, first space station, first successful space rendezvous, first cosmonaut in space, and first cosmonaut staying aboard a space station for more than fourteen months during one trip. She gave a detailed account of Russian cosmonauts' achievements and how her country helped America with its space plans. She was eloquent. Her explication could not have been more lucid. I was greatly impressed with many of the objects on display that were designed to show the country's pioneering space success.

Located at the rear end of the museum, a grand hall boasted a towering dome-shaped ceiling. On the wall, a huge picture of Yuri Gagarin was hanging. He flashes a youthful smile. On the front of his Penguin Suit, there is the design of a dove of peace spreading its wings. He was the first human who turned around to look at the Earth on his journey into outer space. His fellow countrymen had tightened the belts to support the space program. To them, he is a symbol of glory.

What a youthful smile!

The other day I passed by a shoe store. The doors were half open. It was crowded with customers, but none of them were lining up for a service. I saw a young man elbow his way through the crowd to reach the sidewalk. With a smile dancing on his lips, he looked down appreciatively at something he held in his hands. It was a pair of cheap defective shoes.

4

When I left the opera house, it was almost ten o'clock in the evening. While the internal body clock in my brain prepared me for the beginning of night, I found myself pass through the threshold into the mystic lands. The long street was surprisingly quiet. Everything was easily visible. However, sunlight was weak. It had turned grayish, like the pallor in the face of a dying man. It was the midnight sun! For some reason, it reminded me of Sholokhov's *And Quiet Flows the Don* and Dostoyevsky's *Crime and Punishment.* The color painted by midnight was a far cry from sunlight, moonlight, or artificial lighting. It just sent shivers down my spine.

On the sidewalk, there was a lonely man dressed in a full-length overcoat. His silhouette in the pale light disappeared into the distance. At that moment, I completely identified myself with Qu, who used the expression "penetrating chill" all the time when he wrote about his travel experiences in this country.

5

Gigantic, solemn statues of famous literary figures such as Pushkin, Gogol-Yanovski, Gorkii, Tolstoy, Turgenev, Faddeev, and Dostoyevsky, were erected in city parks, public squares, and main streets. I caught a fleeting glimpse of several of them when I was on the bus some distance away. I stood in front of some others, tilting my head to study them carefully. They called to mind the characters the writers had crafted and the sorrow they expressed in their works. This country has produced many of the greatest authors of all time. What kind of path have the Russian people ventured down?

***

Those statues of writers lifting their gaze into the distance or slightly bending the head as if in deep thought are like apertures of the soul of the Russian people. It is unfortunate that my knowledge of them is limited and superficial. After returning home from my trip, I realize that only the paleness of the chilly midnight sun and the image of shoppers stranded in long queues stand out in my memories.

Maybe, what Qu wrote many decades ago no longer holds true today. Still, I want to quote his words to end my essay here:

> Before I came to this country, I had believed that Russia was a laboratory for testing communism. Chemists of the Bolshevik Party used the formulas from the theory of socialism to produce a chemical compound. They combined different elements of the Rus' to make a mixture in the soviet test tube. And then they turned the test tube upside down, shook it quickly, and rocked it vigorously for experimental purposes. However, what I learned from my trip to Siberia convinces me that something might have gone terribly wrong along the way.

October 9, 1987

Eslite for Elites

Eslite Bookstore is every avid reader's dream. As someone from Hong Kong where the love of print is dying, I almost never miss browsing the shop whenever I visit Taipei. The moment I enter it, the soul is liberated. All this may sound a bit far-fetched, but I do feel like an intellectual pilgrim filled with only reverence at the marvel of the Holy Land.

Eslite is the symbol of elegant lifestyle and refined culture. And there is a considerable intellectual pedigree behind its business plan. Recently, the branch on Guangfu S. Road has been running discount promotions. Its publicity flyer reads:

> A FULL DAY'S WORK BEGINS IN THE MORNING
> A sparkling morning is meant to be recovered.
> A leaf the dew rests upon is meant to be kept.
> A bookstore you and I met is meant to be explored.

Meanwhile, the branch on Nanjing Road is launching an advertising campaign. The slogan — "A Warm Book on a Winter Day" — is printed on a piece of square, silver-gray card-paper. From Mondays through Sundays, every day the branch targets on a specific group of customers (like, those who go to work on Sec. 3, Nanjing E. Road or those who are members of the Cloud Gate Dance Theater Club) and provides them with a ten percent discount off the price.

Eslite stays open till midnight. People flip through the pages of a book, quietly enjoying a browser-friendly ambience. Although not everyone decides to make a purchase, there is always a long queue at the cashier. It shows that the marriage of business and cultural activities is still going strong.

Property prices in downtown Taipei are not necessarily cheaper than those in Hong Kong. And Hong Kong magnates are just as well-heeled as their Taiwanese counterparts. But our city is in need of people with vision and ambition, who are capable of seeing how the world could be, and willing to contribute to the creation of engaging places for business-cum-leisure time activities. While our local bookstore owners often complain that their small businesses are operating in the red because of exorbitant rents they are paying, their stores usually swarm with people. It seems that there is a sizeable market for their service. If some people are committed to investing in a business where good books are sold in an appealing ambience, cultivated people will get into the habit of coming in. When the number of customers increases to the point of being noteworthy, book shopping may become an instrument to demonstrate social status. Bookstore owners may even seize the opportunity to achieve their ends by introducing it as a certain kind of "fad" for yuppies.

There is Eslite in Taipei, and there are Forest Song and San Wei in Beijing. It would be nice if there was a similar bookstore in Hong Kong. How about a cozy one with style? We do not want another commercialized bookstore located in a crowded shopping mall. Will our wish remain a pipe dream?

January 21, 1997

Love Seeds

The spring equinox takes place today. The air swells with mist. Outside the window, the Kowloon Peninsula lies before me. Barely visible, now it looks like an extension of the harbor. I sip at a cup of tea. For some reason, memories with coral beans come flooding back.

As a native of the south, I have never seen a coral-bean tree before (although I have read Wang Wei's "Love Seeds"). In their natural habitat, coral-bean trees grow all over the mountains. In spring, once the seeds are mature enough to ripen, they burst the seed coat. The seeds have a lovely coral color. Their decorative pattern is reminiscent of a heart.

There is a tradition that every year when it is time for the locals to peel off their winter coats, a commitment ceremony is held. Young men and women sit together under the coral-bean trees, expecting nothing more than to wait for fate to bring them a soul-mate. When a gentle wind comes up, pods burst open. Hundreds of millions of seeds catch the wind, and drift wherever the wind takes them. Like a shower of pinkish-orange rain falling from the sky, they land in the hair and on the shoulder of those who are waiting for love. If a young man gives one to a woman, and she accepts it, the two of them are committed to a relationship without further ado.

How romantic!

At some time in the past when the Mainland was going through a difficult time, I was inspired to hunt for them. One year in spring, I traveled to Guilin. I asked around in rural areas and in the city to see if anyone knew where coral-bean trees grew. Young people looked at me without understanding what I was talking. They did not have a clue. Older people looked as if they had seen a ghost, and kept shaking their head. At last, I found a white-haired elderly man inside of a dimly lit small shop under a low awning's canopy. He raised his head, and met my gaze. Then he lowered his eyes, and almost murmured to himself in a feeble voice, "All had been cut down. Nothing's left." Why, coral beans were not to be found! After my trip to Guilin, I began to forget the whole thing.

It was not until many years later when I was no longer looking high and low for them that I finally laid my hands on one. The brightly coral-colored seed is shaped like the conventional representation of a heart, even though its two curves are not perfectly symmetrical. It has a deep gloss shine, and looks outrageously delicate against my palm. A friend once suggested that it be turned into a piece of jewelry for everyday wear, like a ring, brooch, or something. However, I resisted the idea. It is not meant to be worn as jewelry. It is a pinkish raindrop from heaven. It is a gift of love. Whatever is yours will come to you eventually.

The love seed is clutched in my fist. When I open my fingers, it clings to my palm where fine creases run across the surface. It looks more exquisite than ever. "When spring draws nearer/How many slender tendrils twine?" I have one love seed, and that is enough for me.

March 26, 1984

A Freehand Sketch of Jiangnan

When I visited Jiangnan[13] this past April, magnolia blossoms opened; plum blossoms opened; cherry blossoms opened. Weeping willows stayed fresh. Flowering peach trees were just coming into bloom (which was later than should have been the case). The scenic view of the West Lake District was as good as it was possible to be. That said, I would have been greatly disappointed if I had not stepped aside from the aesthetic appeal of the Lake to explore other corners of the District, and see it from a whole new humanistic perspective.

Spring was still young.

On a five-kilometer stretch of road, a light wind escorted me into Yangzhou. Clouds over Slender West Lake were thin and high-lying. Willow branches with long tresses swayed gracefully in a slight breeze. I threw on my heavy winter coat, and took a walk along the embankment to enjoy some unusual light-hearted moments. Unlike Du Mu, a leading poet of the Tang Dynasty, I did not bother to find out if the Twenty-Four Bridge still stood today.

Lotus flowers grew on the shallow lake. In calm waters, a bridge was reflected. Under the bridge, a tourist boat drifted by. In the boat, all the sightseers' faces were brightened up with smiles. For sure, small memories collected from their trip would always be remembered. It was a school holiday. School kids in the region were celebrating spring with a picnic. Their laughter and joking echoed through pavilions and pagodas. Dressed in a red tracksuit, they greeted strangers with cheerful hellos, not unlike characters captured in sequences of paintings that bear the unprecedented stamp of a powerful vitality. Yangzhou, once infamous for prostitution, now has a new image.

---

[13] Translator's note: Jiangnan is a geographic area in China referring to the southern part of the Yangtze River.

Luzhi is an old water town located in a city about eighteen kilometers east of Suzhou. "All homes rest their heads on the river's shoulders/There're as many foot bridges as there're water alleys." Morning had just broken. The reflection of sunlight formed a bright, sparkling light on the water ripples. It was the first time I saw sun glitter in my life. Under the Zhengyang Bridge, a woman crouched down at the foot of a set of access steps built into the riverbank. She began to scrub a honey bucket. Yes, you heard me correctly! It was a honey bucket. The hand-made bamboo brush that she used had a long handle. Once scrubbed clean, it is the custom for the locals to leave the (finely-carved) wooden honey bucket along with the brush outside the house, and let them dry in the sun.

Women took their laundry down to the river. Housewives carrying bamboo shopping bags caught up on their gossip in the narrow streets lined with shops established two generations ago. Customers were greeted by a gray-haired jolly hash slinger inside an eating house that served breakfast. Steam was rising from a pot on the stove. I leaned against the white granite parapet of the Hefeng Bridge, my fingers tracing its relief carving designs that had been weathered away over time. This is human existence! I thought. Built at the beginning of the Song Dynasty, the Hefeng Bridge bears witness to the quotidian activities of ordinary people. Their real, uneventful lives in the real world are a vital part of the country's cultural heritage. These days, amusement space such as Han Street and Song Dynasty Town set up in places with scenic views provides a window on the imitation life in ancient China. It would have been nice to upgrade the original households in this water town. Only in this way can a legacy of tradition be kept alive for future generations.

In Luzhi, the locals live life to the fullest in their unhurried manner. Their amiability and gaiety had deeply impressed my mind. Still and all, I felt guilty when I sauntered down a cobbled alleyway. Tourism, in itself, is an act of intrusion and a violation of privacy.

While Luzhi more than fulfilled my expectations, my visit to Longmen Ancient Town was definitely an eye-opener. The Ancient Town lies sixteen kilometers from Fuyang. It is completely captivating.

The guy who gave guided local tours to visitors was quick to reiterate that no one should leave the group during the trip. He did not know his way around the Ancient Town even though he had been there several times. For that reason, he would let a native woman surnamed Sun take the lead. Was it a classic piece of overstatement to say that the Ancient Town is like a maze? All the shadows of doubt dispersed when we entered the foyer of a house, which was the starting point of our tour. The locals have dedicated part of their houses as public right-of-way for alleyways or similar uses that provide access to other places in the neighborhood. Therefore, the tour basically consisted of a house-by-house walk-through of the Ancient Town. One moment we got into the sitting room of a private home, the next we found ourselves in a narrow cobbled passageway. Instead of walking on the street, we spent so much time entering and leaving people's houses that we lost track of our direction. "You walk through the covered alleys to the edge of the town to visit a friend on a rainy day, and when you're back, there isn't even a drop of rain on your shoes," a local spoke proudly about his hometown. Inhabitants in rural areas are renowned for their great hospitality, which rarely exists among urban people in the city.

The Ancient Town showcases to great effect the wooden architecture of the Ming and Qing Dynasties. Posts and beams of large ancestral temples are intricately carved. In particular, the interior of Hundred-Lion Hall is characterized by its supporting beams decorated with lifelike wood carvings of this majestic animal in many positions. Shanle Hall features columns and joists with all kinds of beautiful designs of birds and flowers, and even dialogues of plays. We slowed our hurried pace to feast our eyes on unusual townscapes. It is a pity that ancestral halls had been converted into processing plants where women were doing manufacturing jobs in light industry. Hasn't the Ancient Town been recognized with the official national historic site status? Oh well, one needs to work to live. Over there, a small ancestral shrine was destroyed by fire a few days ago. I surveyed the destruction, and found nothing but rubble and debris. I could imagine it in my mind's eye that a pillar of smoke arose up into the sky, as hand-carved beams embellished with figures of birds and fish and geometric floral patterns were burned into ashes. A farmer passed me as if nothing had happened. A cigarette was hanging from the corner of his mouth.

The traditional gateway lies desolate and in ruins. Does it still serve its purpose of commemorating the ancestors' great achievements? I walked past mud-brick enclosure walls, on which cracks meandered across the surface. I took some pictures of the damaged walls for fear that they would soon be demolished to make way for a theme park like Ming or Qing Dynasty Town. Or, if someone got ants in his pants and decided to do a new coat of red or green paint to cover the old color, then it would be all over.

"Eminences as luxuriously green/As Mount Longmen in Shanxi/Running water fresh and clean/In small rills, delicate streams." I already missed the Ancient Town, even before I said goodbye.

Aside from sightseeing, I was in Jiangnan to watch Kunqu opera.

I am a Kunqu opera lover, although I have but a light superficial knowledge in this kind of musical play. Its subtle singing techniques are said to have been developed in Jiangnan, the most charming region in the country. All my life I have been such a sucker for subtlety, and I am completely crazy about the art of telling without telling. For instance, when an actress just lets a plethora of emotions sink in with a single glance cast over the shoulder, or tucks her loose hair back into place, it goes beyond what words could ever express.

Several highlights from *The Peony Pavilion* were performed by the region's finest actors and actresses. They are members of Suzhou Kunqu Opera Theatre of Jiangsu and Zhejiang Jing Kun Arts Center. Their performances, like "free-flowering plants in a magnificent array of gay colors", appealed to the audience's imagination, and conjured up a diversity of scenes through song and dance.

The best-loved opera was directed by Yao Chuanxiang. Wang Fengmei, who portrayed Du Liniang, the well-depicted character, diligently brought her to life. Her acting techniques of the hand, the eye, the body, and the feet had been developed to absolute perfection, which enabled her to become a fully realized three-dimensional character. This story is about love, dreams and reality, supernatural elements (such as the protagonist's revival), and human vulnerability. On stage, she seamlessly switched between acting styles, depending on what the script demands. Fluidity in movements, and a slight edge of sadness to an otherwise happy sparkle in the eyes communicated just what she meant to communicate – nothing more; nothing less. Indeed, the art of mastering subtlety is a lot more complex than a careless novice actress can imagine. And I became so absorbed in her performance that for a moment I thought that I had hopped a spaceship in Hong Kong. It flew faster than the speed of light, and allowed me to transcend time and space to meet Du Liniang in the Ming Dynasty. In some sense, I was retracting an old dream, just like what Du does in the story. As one of the ancient extant art forms, Kunqu opera may not survive in a new era that is characterized by cultural turbulence. People in the hectic modern world have a memory like a sieve. They come up with all kinds of excuses why customs and traditions should be swept under the rug. As it happens, such a worrying thought keeps nagging at both performers and audiences these days.

Much as Jiangnan has been the most written about region in the country over the past millennium, there is always something new to discover. Before the trip, I had envisaged this la-la land of dreams much more sensual and sublime. Upon my return, I realize that it was just wishful thinking. But, when all is said and done, I am a city person. A city person is only meant to handle rural life in small bursts.

April, 1996

A Rendezvous with Spring in Jiangnan

If you plan to visit Jiangnan and ask me for travel tips, I do have a lot to say.

Here is a list of the top things to do in the West Lake District. Listen to the ringing of the Nanping bell in the early evening. Go to a park where orioles sing and willows wave. Take a stroll on the Xiling Bridge. Visit Feilai Peak (legend has it that the Peak had flown over from a faraway country). Yue Fei Temple is also a tourist attraction. When I was there in tougher political times several years ago, I asked an old man for directions to the mausoleum but was stonewalled. He was afraid to get into trouble. And if you get a chance to visit that place, you will notice that the statues of General Yue Fei and his enemy, Qin Hui, have been re-carved. A new leaf of history is turned over.

Naturally, shade gardens in Suzhou just call to mind the quintessential tragic love story of Jia Baoyu and Lin Daiyu from A Dream of the Red Chamber. And Cold Mountain Temple is a must-see religious site, where the stroke of midnight is celebrated by ringing great bells.

You cannot go to Nanjing and not see Stone City (where all that remains are only portions of an ancient city wall), and the Qinhuai River (where still waters are agitated by the revolution of modernization). In souvenir shops, you can find stone fragments taken from Yuhua Hill. Heavily weathered, they are witnesses to a troubling and violent past in the country.

And it is impossible to see and do everything when you visit Taihu Lake and Mochou Lake. You must stand prepared to behold some bewitching scenery. So, here are some ideas to get you started!

Go see the fallen tears of dawn gleaming on fresh, bewitching willows; the moving blades of young grass grown among mosses on tiled roofs; a few empty boats rising and falling on the ebb tide; and a young bird spreading its wings for the first time.

Walk down a cobbled alleyway. You hear an early riser open a wood door leaving his house for work. He carries something in his hand while wheeling his bicycle by his side. It is just an ordinary day in his life. He is just an ordinary person whose name you do not know, and whose face you will not remember. When you pass him, say hi to him in exchange for a sunny smile if you are willing.

At the fording place of the river, there are usually several people doing laundry, most of them are women. Their pants legs are rolled high. Crouching on the steps by the riverside, they beat and wash clothes. They chat occasionally to catch up on all the gossip.

When you visit sites of antiquity, you can never be sure that the history you know is authentic. Well, there is much interpretation built into any historical analysis. But one thing is for sure, spring puts in an appearance every year without fail. When she arrives, you are better off visiting Jiangnan for a taste of local life.

"In Jiangnan if you catch up with spring/Kindly find a way to make her stay." This quote is for you. Keep it in your heart when you go on your trip.

March 28, 1980

The Madam White Snake series will see the light of day in summer, 2019. Get a sneak preview into *A Debt of Love*!

Mount Emei is a sacred mountain in Sichuan Province, China.

It was not one of the five most renowned mountains in Chinese history, but it had a well-deserved reputation for being a place of enlightenment. In the depths of the mountain, there was a cave used by a white-snake sprite as a lair. During the past few hundred years, it cultivated its vital energy by getting nutrients from sunbeams, moonlight, zephyrs, and heaven's breath. Now it was on the verge of shape-shifting into a human being.

One evening, the glare of the bright moon lit up the cloudless sky. The white-snake sprite peeked out of the cave's entrance. It saw a light pillar shooting down from the sky. A mystic red *dan* floated in the air. It was a crystalline substance where the three treasures of life essence, vital energy, and soul found residence.

The white-snake sprite lifted its gaze. It spotted an elderly Buddhist monk sitting with his legs crossed, practicing meditation halfway up the mountain. For all it knew, he was a toad sprite in human form. He had been living in the neighborhood for a long time, but did not earn much respect from others for his conduct. This evening, he coincidentally happened to spit out his dan. It was the first time the white-snake sprite saw one. Now it was dangling no more than three meters above its head.

Temptation was harder to resist than it thought. Without warning, the white-snake sprite coiled its body and lunged toward it. It inhaled deeply. With a strong suck, it drew the dan into the mouth. Then it beat a hasty retreat to its lair, hanging the monk out to dry.

For the monk, having his dan stolen by the white-snake sprite was disastrous. He had spent the past five hundred years developing superpowers, but now his work went down the drain. Luckily, when it came to tapping into inner energy, he was in a class of his own. At this moment, he just had to bite the bullet and go back to square one. But he was hoping that their paths would cross again in the near future. He would seize the opportunity to get even with it for that.

And the monk's loss was the white-snake sprite's gain. After swallowing his dan, it entered the flesh of a stunningly beautiful woman. She named herself Suzhen. Ordinarily, she enjoyed a leisurely ramble in the countryside. One day, she was out collecting wild flowers and medicinal herbs. She caught sight of a Taoist nun standing in the middle of a swirl of advection fog, whose face was calm and serene.

Suzhen knew right away that she was a deity. She walked up to the nun and introduced herself. The nun took one look at her and she had been made. It was true enough that Suzhen was a sprite in female form, but she was neither evil nor malicious. She had never killed an innocent before.

"My name's Ruizhi. I'm from West Tarn. I'm a pupil of Empress Jinci," the deity said.

Suzhen knelt down without hesitation. She pleaded with the deity to accept her as her disciple. Her sincerity moved Ruizhi. She gave Suzhen a new name – Liuzhi, and took her home.

Did you like this excerpt? Stay tuned.

The Lost Tales of Hong Kong

Lightning Source UK Ltd.
Milton Keynes UK
UKHW010631260420
362312UK00001B/84